"I met Brian Blount on one of t [amazed] by the anointing on Brian's life and the level of faith for healing. He is the real deal, powerfully anointed, full of faith and bold outside the church, not just within it. *Putting Jesus on Display with Love and Power* is an important book for those wanting or needing to be encouraged to engage in evangelism that rests upon the power of God rather than on the wisdom of man. Practical, inspirational and valuable. I strongly endorse it."

Randy Clark, D.Min., overseer, Apostolic Network of Global
Awakening; president, Global Awakening Theological Seminary;
author, *Power to Heal, The Healing Breakthrough,
There Is More!* and *Baptized in the Holy Spirit*

"Brian Blount is inspiring, as is his book *Putting Jesus on Display with Love and Power.* Be aware, this book goes beyond inspiration. Brian is what I call a practical theologian. He not only teaches the Bible, but demonstrates it and teaches us how to put it into practice. Jesus came to put an invisible God on display. Brian through this book shows us how to put Jesus on display!"

Bob Hazlett, author, *The Roar: God's Sound in a Raging World*;
www.bobhazlett.org

"Brian Blount's passion for releasing God's love and power, along with his strength in equipping and releasing everyone into the ministry of Jesus, is evident throughout this book. What is most impressive about Brian is that he sees these miracles right where he lives—on the streets of his city, on the phone or over the internet—as God's power flows through him. This book will give you the encouragement you need to 'step across the chicken line' and move into the joy of purpose fulfilled."

Dr. Mike Hutchings, director of education,
Global School of Supernatural Ministry,
Global Certification Programs, Global Awakening

"If an ordinary Jesus-loving father of six can regularly pray for people to be healed at the drive-thru, in a shopping mall and on Uber rides, then so can you! This is the message *and* the lifestyle of Brian Blount. Brian is the real deal in every way and has done a meticulous job of documenting his many adventures, including both successes and failures. Read and be encouraged that you, too, can put Jesus on display every day."

Dianne Leman, founding senior pastor,
The Vineyard Church of Central Illinois

"I love Brian for his humanity, humility, honesty and lack of hype. He lives a lifestyle of putting Jesus on display and is passionately committed to training and equipping others to do the same. This book is, quite simply, the best practical how-to guide I've read concerning power evangelism. I plan to recommend it to everyone within my sphere of influence. Thank you, Brian, for reminding us that every follower of Jesus is called to put Jesus on display with love and power."

Jack Moraine, senior pastor, Vineyard Gilbert (Arizona);
southwest regional leader, Vineyard USA

"This book resonates with the real-life story of a disciple of Jesus and practitioner of the Kingdom who lives in all the struggles and challenges of our frail humanity, yet who allows the triumph of the Gospel to shine through despite those often hard realities. Further, Brian is a practitioner who is always putting himself out there in the place of risk. Finally, it beckons every Christian to be a radical and risk-taking disciple of Jesus."

Dr. Derek Morphew, theological consultant, Vineyard Institute

"It seems every generation needs a clarion call to continue the empowered ministry of Jesus establishing the Kingdom of God on earth. For me and my generation, it came through the paradigm-shifting message and ministry of John Wimber. Brian Blount's new book echoes that clear call to this generation. Through clear and balanced teaching, moving testimonies, a very user-friendly model of ministry and Brian's heartfelt compassion, this book awakens a deep desire to live a life that looks like Jesus. It certainly did in my heart!"

Ed Piorek, author, *The Father Loves You* and *Classic Vineyard*

"More than just about anyone else I know, Brian Blount lives in the regular experience of the miraculous. His down-to-earth personality, accessible style of equipping, and inspiring testimonies open up walking in the power of the Spirit to so many—whether our first response is to find that idea exciting or intimidating. I love *Putting Jesus on Display with Love and Power* because it is filled with both the tools and the inspiration to live the as-you-go lifestyle that Brian so powerfully portrays!"

Putty Putman, senior executive pastor, The Vineyard Church of Central Illinois; author, *Kingdom Impact*

"It's the birthright of every believer to see the Kingdom advance through our heart and hands. My friend Brian Blount lives that reality. His partnership with Jesus is simple and beautiful. It's also powerful. But the best part is that it's available to everyone. This is an accessible, helpful book for ordinary believers seeking to release the power of the Kingdom wherever they go. Packed with remarkable stories, each page stirs hope, builds faith and puts Jesus on display!"

Alan Scott, pastor, Vineyard Anaheim

"Courageous faith is what this remarkable book is all about. It's difficult to describe the impact this book has had on me, other than to say that I long more than ever to pray for and minister to those who are suffering with a courageous, risk-taking, relentless faith in the goodness, greatness and power of God. If you read this book, and do so with an open heart and an inquiring mind, your faith in what God can do today will expand and deepen immeasurably. I highly recommend it."

Sam Storms, Bridgeway Church, Oklahoma City

"If you love reading adventure and faith, then this book that Brian Blount has penned is going to have you engaged and excited to be on the lookout. As usual, Brian is simply telling stories, and following a rich tradition, he makes God out to be the constant hero! If you're a pilgrim on a journey, this read will encourage you to pay attention to all the divine nudges."

Phil Strout, national director, Vineyard USA

"This is an important motivational book in the best sense. We seriously need to recover the risk-taking faith of reaching people daily with the compassionate love of Jesus in the supernatural power of His Spirit. Brian Blount conveys the heart, the mind and the practice of power evangelism. Grounded in a sound biblical theology of the Kingdom, this book illustrates each principle of power evangelism with inspiring stories of real-life happenings with Jesus, 'as you go, wherever you go.' This is a great read!"

Alexander Venter, pastor, Association of Vineyard Churches; international teacher; author, *Doing Church* and *Doing Healing*

"Brian Blount and his team were nothing short of amazing when they came to my concerts to help me love on the many rock-'n'-roll fans in attendance. Their nonjudgmental attitude was very encouraging and inspiring. God's Spirit moved in healings, prophetic words and the reality of God's existence, and love was displayed in a very tangible way. I wholeheartedly recommend *Putting Jesus on Display with Love and Power* because I've seen it in action at my concerts, and the impact was completely undeniable!"

Brian "Head" Welch, co-founder of the rock band Korn; author, *Stronger*, *With My Eyes Wide Open* and *New York Times* bestseller *Save Me from Myself*

PUTTING JESUS ON DISPLAY WITH LOVE AND POWER

PUTTING JESUS ON DISPLAY

WITH
LOVE AND POWER

BRIAN BLOUNT

Chosen

a division of Baker Publishing Group
Minneapolis, Minnesota

Published by Chosen Books
11400 Hampshire Avenue South
Bloomington, Minnesota 55438
www.chosenbooks.com

Chosen Books is a division of
Baker Publishing Group, Grand Rapids, Michigan

Printed in the United States of America

Library of Congress Cataloging-in-Publication Data
Names: Blount, Brian K., author.
Title: Putting Jesus on display with love and power / Brian Blount.
Description: Minneapolis : Chosen Books, a division of Baker Publishing
    Group, 2019.
Identifiers: LCCN 2019019609 | ISBN 9780800799304 (trade paper : alk. paper)
    | ISBN 9781493418800 (e-book)
Subjects: LCSH: Christian life. | Supernatural.
Classification: LCC BV4501.3 .B573 2019 | DDC 248.4—dc23
LC record available at https://lccn.loc.gov/2019019609

Note that in some of the author's stories, the names and identifying details of certain individuals have been changed to protect their privacy.

19 20 21 22 23 24 25   7 6 5 4 3 2 1

Dedicated to my six children, Annalisa, Tyler, Amberlyn, Josiah, Nathaniel and Ashley. My prayer is that you would always know how much I love and treasure you. But even more than that, I pray you would always know the love of the Father, and through that, you would live a lifestyle of putting Jesus on display.

CONTENTS

FOREWORD

In 2011, I was speaking in Russia at a training event for a de-nomination's missions department. One of the other facilitators, Charles Bello, kept saying to me, "You've got to meet Brian Blount. You both do the same stuff. . . ." He later handed me a book he had co-authored with Brian, called *From the Sanctuary to the Streets*. Reading about Brian's faith for ministering healing and his passion for equipping others to do the same had such an impact on me. As I read about his journey of being impacted by Blaine Cook (a man who had an impact on me as well, and actually at the same meeting as Brian), I knew that Brian and I were connected. I instantly became a fan of Brian Blount.

Brian has a passion like few I have seen to equip all the Body of Christ to walk in the fullness of who Christ is. In this book, he so powerfully communicates "putting Jesus on display," the truth that we the Church have a calling and responsibility not just to believe the words of Scripture, but actually to walk in them. Putting Jesus on display is not just a teaching. It is a powerful and dynamic invitation to step out of "normal" life and into the supernatural life that Christ and the disciples themselves lived. Brian's gift goes beyond just inviting you to hear his stories of healing and the miraculous. You will actually receive an impartation from them as you read this book.

Brian speaks with such power because he completely remains his normal self, while seeing incredible supernatural activity on a daily basis. Don't get me wrong—his stories will captivate you and show you a high level of supernatural power. But Brian's honest, simplistic approach and communication style gives you the understanding and permission to go and do the same as he does by remaining who you naturally are. When I read this book, I feel the faith to go and see people jump out of wheelchairs, and to see blind eyes open, yet I also feel the peace to go out and fail big in the effort of "going for it."

"Why?" you ask.

Because Brian gives us the realization that living the book of Acts and putting Jesus on display is demonstrated both in the blind eye opening, and in it not opening while I am trying—because I am obeying Christ in His instructions to go. Reading Brian's words, you will be freed from your fear of failure and empowered to witness the miraculous by your own words and your own hands, but with Christ's very own power.

Brace for impact, and hear the call in these pages to "put Jesus on display" everywhere you go.

Robby Dawkins, documentary film subject; bestselling author and
international conference speaker; robbydawkins.com

ACKNOWLEDGMENTS

Thank you to my wife, Jeanine, for helping me put my words together on paper in a way that communicates my thoughts and history with the Lord well, and for encouraging me through the entire process. This book would never have happened without you. Thank you to my children, who are the most important part of my day. You have also sacrificed as I have taken time to write this book, and you have sacrificed as I have traveled in ministry.

Many thanks to Jeanine's parents, Jack and Bonnie Spratt, who are the best Mimi and Papa in the world. You love our children well, and you have taken the kids for several weekends so Jeanine and I could get away to work on this project. It could not have happened without your support.

Thank you also to Charles Bello, who has been my friend, mentor, pastor and sounding board, supporting me through the trials and joys of ministry for over twenty years. You offered valuable ideas, feedback and encouragement as I was writing this book.

I'd also like to thank my friend Blaine Cook. God used you in a profound way that changed my life forever. You helped me believe that the Holy Spirit wanted to empower even me—just an ordinary believer who was hungry to see the Kingdom come—and that I, too, could live out a naturally supernatural lifestyle. Thank you for your faithfulness to steward what God gave you, model it for others and give it away.

1

DEAF EARS OPENING

Jesus, I want to see the deaf hear tonight.

This is a prayer I have prayed many times, but this evening in Brazil it seemed to carry a special weight. I was reminded of Isaiah 35:5, the Scripture that says, "Then will the eyes of the blind be opened and the ears of the deaf unstopped." We had seen the blind see on that trip, but my heart was yearning to see the deaf hear, too. I wanted to put Jesus on display by doing the ministry He called every believer to do. And that includes healing the deaf.

A month previously, I had been ministering at a church in the United States when a young girl asked for prayer. She had been born without any ear at all on one side—it had been folded in on itself, and there was no shape of an outer ear and apparently none of the structures inside the ear that allow hearing to take place. Plastic surgeons had created an outer ear for her, but it was purely cosmetic. She had undergone surgery to help her doctors determine if hearing would be possible through a medical hearing device. The outlook was dismal outside of supernatural healing.

As I began to pray for this girl, I could feel a spirit of unbelief settle all around me. I could feel it trying to creep up inside me, to keep me from praying. I could feel it coming from the demonic forces that know a seed of unbelief can squelch out the conviction that Jesus still heals today and uses everyday people like you and me to do it.

It would have been so easy to launch into the "sometimes we don't see healing happen, and sometimes Jesus heals gradually" speech, but instead I prayed for her. I prayed a quick, short prayer of command, telling the malformed ear to hear. I prayed again and again. Each time I prayed, I asked the girl to test out her ear and see if she noticed any difference. Gradually, she started hearing faint sounds. Then louder sounds. Within moments, she could hear fully on both sides!

She wept as she covered her good ear and others whispered into the opposite ear, which had lacked the necessary structures for hearing anything. She wept again as she held a phone up and had a conversation through an ear that had been impossible to hear through.

That evening in Brazil, as I prayed, *Jesus, I want to see the deaf hear tonight*, I recalled that girl's face from a month earlier, beaming in the wonder of God's goodness.

I had been in Brazil for a couple of weeks, ministering with my good friend Blaine Cook, and we had joined up with Randy Clark and his Global Awakening ministry trip to Brazil. That evening it was Blaine's turn to speak, and I would be part of the ministry team. I had seen God do amazing things on this trip—there had been tremendous healings and outpouring of God's power. But I had yet to see the deaf hear.

As we pulled up to the church in our bus, the prayer rose inside me again: *I want to see the deaf hear tonight*. When I walked into the building, I noticed a section reserved for the deaf ministry, something I had not seen at all in my weeks in Brazil. My faith skyrocketed. I knew that it was not just my prayer I had been praying. It was the Lord giving me faith. He was showing me what He wanted to do that evening. He wanted to heal the deaf.

At the end of the service I began ministering to people, but I was struggling because of the language barrier. I don't speak Portuguese, and not many people spoke English. A woman named Ana approached me. "Do you need help? I could interpret for you," she offered. She explained hesitantly that she had never interpreted before, but she was willing to try.

We began praying for people, and amazing things were happening. Ana wept as we saw more and more people healed of various illnesses and pains. She had never seen healings like this. I began coaching her in how she could pray for the sick on her own. She was amazed that people were getting healed through her hands. And yet my heart was yearning for the deaf section on the other side of the room.

"Ana," I asked, "do you mind if we go over to the deaf section? Do you think any of the people there would like us to pray for them?" Not only did I not know Portuguese, I also certainly did not know how to sign. I knew I would definitely need Ana's assistance to enlist the help of the people who were signing, who could translate for us.

"Let me go ask," she said. She walked over to the deaf section, and to my astonishment, she began to sign with them. Ana knew Brazilian Sign Language! At that moment, I knew something supernatural was about to happen. That prayer I had been praying as I pulled up on the bus had come from God's heart. What are the odds of being offered the help of someone who could interpret in English, Portuguese and sign language? This had to be a divine appointment. As Ana asked the people with deafness if anyone wanted prayer for healing, one lady quickly came forward.

I have a strong conviction that the ministry of Jesus is supposed to be reproducible and meant for all believers, not just a select few anointed disciples. Ana translated from English into Portuguese and Brazilian Sign Language, and I coached her as we both prayed for this woman's hearing to be restored. We prayed three or four times, each time with the woman's hearing beginning to open more and more. Eventually, her ears popped open and she could hear fully. She had been born deaf in both ears, so she had never heard anything. She did not yet have the ability to speak, but she could hear!

Tears were streaming down the woman's face, and her eyes beamed with awe and joy. "It's so loud!" she signed to Ana as noises she had never heard overwhelmed her.

Immediately, the woman wanted to find her husband and share what had happened. He was also deaf from birth, and she thought, *If my ears can be opened, maybe his can, too.* She signed to Ana, asking if she could bring him over and we could pray.

I told her through Ana, "We would love to pray for your husband, but I want you to help us pray!"

Ana and I then showed the woman how to help us pray for her husband. To her amazement, Jesus used her to help bring healing to him. The sweetest thing to me was that she was pregnant. These new parents would now be able to hear their baby's cries and respond. They would learn their child's voice. They would rejoice at his or her first words. A whole new world had just opened up to them.

We continued praying for more people in the deaf section. Each time someone was healed and could hear for the first time, I had that person pray with me for the next person. Jesus said in Matthew 10:8, "Freely you have received; freely give." I was explaining in English, Ana was interpreting into Brazilian Sign Language, and then the now-hearing, formerly deaf people would help pray for their friends.

Another woman who had been born deaf had a husband who was not deaf. When he learned what had happened, he came up behind her and whispered in her ear. To his shock, she turned around at the sound of his voice, which she had heard for the first time! They embraced with tears of joy rolling down their cheeks.

Jesus was not only restoring hearing to her; He was bringing a deeper intimacy that this couple had never experienced before to their marriage.

"I've never seen anything like this," exclaimed the man who led the church's deaf ministry. He was stunned as he went around to check on each of the people as they were healed, to make sure they could hear. I prayed for him and Ana for an increased impartation for healing, and the power of God came strongly upon both of them.

"I think your ministry to the deaf has just changed," I told them. "Not only will you minister to them through sign language interpretation, but now your ministry will also include healing them!" Their lives were radically changed that night, too.

In all, six people who had never heard from birth were healed and received full ability to hear. That night, there had been a total of twelve people in the deaf section. I am convinced that the other six would have been healed, too, except that they had already left by the time Ana and I made it over to their section.

When I got back on the bus, I sat there in awe and wonder, reflecting on what had happened. Not only did we see hundreds of healings, my little prayer earlier on the bus to see the deaf hear was also answered beyond what I could have imagined. We had seen a fulfillment of Isaiah 35:5, "Then the eyes of the blind will be opened and the ears of the deaf unstopped."

Six months later, I was ministering in South Africa. One of the difficulties I encounter there (and in most other places as well) is not a lack of faith that God will heal, but a lack of understanding that God will heal through ordinary believers. Although they believe in the anointing on "the man of God" to heal, often Christians don't think God can use *them*.

It was this lack of understanding I was confronting at a church service in South Africa when I said, "I know you all believe that God can heal people through me. But you don't believe God could use you to heal the sick. You also don't believe God could use the sick to heal the sick. You think you are disqualified because you have sickness. Both of those are lies from the enemy. God has called every believer to heal the sick, and He can even use the sick to heal the sick. You don't believe it yet, but you're going to believe it. Who here has a deaf ear on one side?"

Two women stood up and came forward. One woman had been deaf in one ear for a couple of years, and the other had been deaf on one side for much longer. I had the women face each other as I said to the congregation, "As a sign to you that God will use ordinary people, and that God can use the sick to heal the sick, I'm going to have these ladies pray for each other. As soon as they do, their deaf ears will completely open!"

As soon as the words were out of my mouth, I felt uncertain. It had been a gift of faith that had given me the boldness to make such a confident declaration, but now I was struggling. I thought to myself, *Either something supernatural is going to happen or I'm going to be humbled, and I'm okay with either of those outcomes.*

I instructed the ladies, "Place your hand on each other's deaf ear and simply command the deafness to leave."

As they did this, immediately both their deaf ears opened. The congregation was stunned. And I have to admit, I was stunned, too! These seemingly unanointed, broken, deaf ladies had prayed for each other, and both of them had received their hearing instantly.

This demonstration of God's desire to use every ordinary believer to do the ministry of Jesus shifted the church. The result was a congregation of people who believed they could heal the sick. That evening, as a line of people who needed healing stretched from one end of the church to the other, 100 percent of them received healing, all through the hands of other people in their own congregation who believed Jesus wanted to use them. That night clearly demonstrated that it is not about the man of God; it is about the people of God.

It is not just physical deafness that Jesus wants to heal. He also wants to heal our spiritual deafness. As Jesus proclaimed, "He who has ears to hear, let him hear!" (Matthew 11:15 NKJV). I believe that what happened that day in South Africa was a prophetic sign to all of them, but also to all of us. Jesus wants to use everyone—even you—to put Him on display.

I believe a spiritual deafness has fallen over much of the Church today. It is a deafness that has kept people from hearing and believing that God has called every believer to put Jesus on display with signs and wonders. This spiritual deafness has blocked the ears of believers from hearing the commission He gave us. I believe this spiritual deafness has perpetuated the lie of the evil one that causes people to think, *God can't use me.* Or, *I'm not qualified; it's only for an anointed few people.* Or, *These gifts have passed away.* This spiritual deafness has blocked us from hearing Jesus' commissioning to His Church (all believers): "As you go, proclaim this message: 'The kingdom of heaven has come near.' Heal the sick, raise the dead, cleanse those who have leprosy, drive out demons. Freely you have received; freely give" (Matthew 10:7–8).

We have all been commissioned to heal the sick, preach the good news of the Kingdom and demonstrate the love and power of God to those around us. It is not about possessing a special gifting or anointing. It is not about the great man or woman of God. It is about the great God of men.

I believe God has given us ears for the purpose of hearing, not only physically, but also spiritually. We as the Church and the people of God need to have ears to hear what the Spirit of the Lord is saying, in order that we might put Jesus on display with love and power.

2

JESUS' MISSION, MESSAGE AND MINISTRY

One of my greatest mentors was a man I never met: John Wimber. He was the founder of the Vineyard movement and a man who taught people across many cultures and denominations how to put Jesus on display with love and power. I learned from him by watching hours of his ministry on VHS tapes, listening to him on cases of cassette tapes and reading everything of his I could. Wimber coined the term *power evangelism* and wrote a book by that name. He appealed to the Spirit-empowered ethos of the Pentecostal Church and the biblical focus of the evangelical Church. He demystified spiritual gifts and gave practical and implementable models that believers from varied ecclesial backgrounds could embrace. The foundation of Wimber's theological teachings, coupled with practical models, shaped my understanding of what it means to put Jesus on display.

Power evangelism is the empowering work of the Holy Spirit on the believer, released through the gifts of the Spirit such as healing, prophecy, the casting out of demons, raising the dead and releasing the tangible, manifest presence of the Spirit. It empowers a disciple with the ability to proclaim and demonstrate the good news of the Gospel. In other words, power evangelism is simply learning to partner with the Holy Spirit to do what Jesus did. It is relying on the Spirit, not on our own ability.

Power evangelism is illustrated in the life of Jesus and the disciples, and throughout the gospels and the book of Acts, as well as through all of Church history to the present. Looking at the life and ministry of Jesus and His disciples, I believe power evangelism is the most biblical approach to evangelism. There are other forms that are very important, but we must press in for the Spirit-empowered proclamation and demonstration of the good news of the Gospel. As believers, we are called to do what Jesus did. He engaged the world by healing the sick, casting out demons and even raising the dead.

For the believer, Jesus is the center of everything we do in life and ministry. Through the gospel accounts, we see an astounding picture of His ministry. We see His kindness and compassion; we hear His message of salvation for all of humanity. Not only did He preach the Good News, He was also very hands-on about demonstrating that Good News. We see Him teaching the multitudes and also multiplying food through the hands of His disciples for those hungry crowds. He shared the mysteries of the Kingdom of God while also curing diseases. As followers of Jesus, we must learn His style of doing ministry.

To understand how and why Jesus did what He did, we need to understand His *mission, message, means, method* and *model* for ministry. I call these the 5 M's of Jesus' ministry. I know others have put together similar lists, but I have developed this particular list collaboratively with my mentor, Charles Bello, and it has evolved over the years into these 5 M's. They are the anchors that ground us in Jesus. In order to put Him on display, we must first and foremost be students of what Jesus actually taught, demonstrated and imparted to His disciples and to us today. With that in mind, let's look at each of these more closely.

Jesus' Mission: Isaiah 61

Jesus began His public ministry at the age of thirty. He had spent the previous years as an unknown carpenter from an insignificant family in a small town near the Sea of Galilee. But after His baptism in the Jordan River and forty days of fasting and trial in the wilderness, Jesus made a pretty startling debut onto the public scene.

Luke 4:14 tells us that Jesus returned from the wilderness "in the power of the Spirit, and news about him spread through the whole countryside." He made His way back to His hometown of Nazareth and went to the synagogue to worship on the Sabbath. This is the same synagogue He had grown up in from the time He was a child. These people knew Him. They knew His family. They thought of Him as a normal Jewish carpenter.

It was Jesus' turn to read from the Scriptures on this particular Sabbath day. When He was handed the scroll of the book of Isaiah, He made a poignant choice. Out of all the passages He could have chosen in this massive book, He selected Isaiah 61. The crowd knew exactly what this Scripture was. It was well established that this passage was a prophetic word about the coming Messiah—the Savior who would come to redeem Israel and all of humanity. It was this passage Jesus began to read aloud:

> The Spirit of the Lord is on me, because he has anointed me to proclaim good news to the poor. He has sent me to proclaim freedom for the prisoners and recovery of sight for the blind, to set the oppressed free, to proclaim the year of the Lord's favor.
>
> Luke 4:18–19

As if selecting this passage were not a bold enough move, He did not stop there. "Today this scripture is fulfilled in your hearing," He declared (verse 21). He went on to describe how the prophets of old were rejected by those in their hometowns. Jesus the carpenter had thrown down the gauntlet. And the crowd was infuriated by his claims.

Not only was Jesus saying He was the Messiah, He also was declaring His mission statement. He had come to proclaim good news to the poor, to proclaim freedom for the prisoners and recovery of sight for the blind, to set the oppressed free and to proclaim the year of the Lord's favor. From that day on, this statement became the mission He lived His life by.

Jesus came from heaven to earth on a mission. The Father sent Him to the world out of love. John 3:16–18 tells us that God so loved the world that He gave His Son. And Jesus said that He did not come to condemn the world, for it was already condemned. He came to save the world (see John 12:47). He comes with the power of heaven into the earth to show us how much we and others are loved.

The mission of Luke 4:18–19 tells us that Jesus came to proclaim good news to the poor. He was speaking of far more than only a financial poverty; He was speaking of the poverty of the human soul. Jesus came to show us that we are not orphans. There is a Father in heaven who loves us. Though we may be spiritually bankrupt, Jesus came to set everything right and to bring us into connection and communion with the Father. The Spirit was on Jesus for that purpose. Jesus demonstrated the reality of that by recovering sight for the blind (spiritually and physically), and by releasing the oppressed and those people who were bound.

We are surrounded by this mission field every day. When we go to work or school, we see oppressed people and those who are blinded by the god of this world. The Spirit of the Lord came on Jesus to release them, and the Spirit is meant to come on us for the same purpose. As we go about our days as followers of Jesus, His mission is to be our mission. His job description is our job description. We, too, have been commissioned to live by the mission to proclaim good news to the poor, proclaim freedom for the prisoners and recovery of sight for the blind, to set the oppressed free and to proclaim the year of the Lord's favor.

Let me illustrate it this way. Imagine for a moment that two thousand years ago, Jesus came to the earth to be a great baseball player. If Jesus' mission had been to play baseball, what is the first thing He would have done? Baseball is not a one-man sport, so He would have been scouting Israel for more baseball players. Certainly, He could have looked for the great players of the day to recruit to His team. He could have gone to the great White Sox Pharisee Stadium to find the pros. But that is not what Jesus did. Instead, He went to the dilapidated fields and back alleys, where sticks and homemade balls were more likely to be found than handcrafted bats and regulation baseballs. He walked up to an overgrown field full of ragtag men who were not even playing baseball. They were playing tee-ball. He saw Peter with a bat in his hand, ready to swing at the head of the next person who ticked him off. Thomas was doubting if they would ever graduate from the tee to a real pitcher. James and John were in a brawl, fighting over who was the greatest tee-ball player on the team, while Judas snuck around stealing from the concession stand.

I can just see Jesus looking up to the Big Coach in heaven and questioning, *These are the guys?*

And the answer was, *Yes, these are the guys.* So Jesus shouted out to the players, "Hey! Drop your tee-ball equipment and follow Me. I'm going to teach you to be great baseball players."

Jesus gathered His new team around Him and picked up His Great Baseball Manual. He turned to Coach Isaiah and read, "For the Spirit of the Big Coach is upon Me! He has anointed Me to teach and play baseball. He has sent Me to hit home runs, to catch fly balls, to strike out the enemy team, to free those on the bases and to declare that this is the year we will win the World Series!"

Over the next weeks and months, Jesus began to teach these guys how to play baseball. He coached them on how to swing the bat, catch fly balls and throw spitballs. He showed them strategy and technique they had never imagined before. Not only was Jesus a great baseball player Himself; He also developed a team of baseball players. And it did not stop there. His baseball team went on to develop other baseball teams, and the glory of baseball spread throughout the land.

Fast-forward two thousand years later. Every once in a while, we still open up our Baseball Manuals. We reminisce about all the great baseball games that used to be. We celebrate the baseball revivals of the past. We are fascinated by the techniques of our ancient baseball heroes. We get caught up in speculating about the Anti-Coach who will come to try to destroy the game. We buy tickets to watch others play ball. We even criticize the players on the field and talk about how they should play better. But we never step up to the plate, swing our bats and play Kingdom ball.

Jesus had a mission, and it was not to play baseball. His mission statement said that the Spirit of the Lord was upon Him for a purpose. It was to heal the sick and set the captives free. It was to bring sight to the blind and liberty to the oppressed. Rather than walking in the reality of Jesus' mission, today we find ourselves in the stands, watching others play the game. We have been sidelined voluntarily and have made ourselves comfortable spectators.

It is time to step out of the spectator stands and get into the game. It is time to take Jesus' mission seriously and realize that the Great Commission did not end with the disciples; it had just begun. We are still called to duplicate Jesus' mission today.

Jesus' Message: The Kingdom Is at Hand

Not only did Jesus have a mission, He also had a message: *The Kingdom of God is at hand*. Jesus repeats this phrase constantly, along with its twin statement: *The Kingdom of heaven has come near*. This message was His primary preaching topic and was the language He chose to use to communicate God's activity.

The crowds around Jesus were weary from decades of Roman occupation. They were desperate to be once again an autonomous nation outside the bounds of invading foreign forces. They wanted to see the throne of David reestablished, and they anticipated a Messiah who would institute the rule and reign of God back in Israel. So when Jesus said the Kingdom of God is at hand, it had to seem bewildering to this audience. Jesus used the phrase often, but no military changes were happening. No foreign political despots were falling. Rather, the blind were seeing. The demon-possessed were freed. The hungry were fed. The lame walked. Yes, the Kingdom of God was at hand!

God's Kingdom cannot be confined to political borders or military conquests. His Kingdom is established where His will is being accomplished. The reaches of His Kingdom are everywhere the rule and reign of the King is being executed. God's rule and reign had come in the person of Jesus, who preached that the Kingdom of God is at hand, right here. It is not out of reach, too far away to attain. It is as close as your own hand.

Matthew 4:23–24 summarizes Jesus' activity this way:

> Jesus went throughout Galilee, teaching in their synagogues, proclaiming the good news of the kingdom, and healing every disease and sickness among the people. News about him spread all over Syria, and people brought to him all who were ill with various diseases, those suffering severe pain, the demon-possessed, those having seizures, and the paralyzed; and he healed them.

In other words, God's rule and reign—His Kingdom—was at hand.

Jesus' message of the Kingdom carried power. It declared freedom from the real oppression around the people—oppression that kept humanity and all of creation in captivity. As they were set free, Jesus would declare that the Kingdom had come upon them (see Matthew 12:28; Luke 11:20).

Jesus also commissioned His disciples to preach this same message. He did not keep it to Himself, but gave it to His followers. Before His disciples embarked on ministry, He instructed them in Matthew 10:7, "As you go, proclaim this message: 'The kingdom of heaven has come near.'" So not only has Jesus' mission become our mission, His message is also our message. The Kingdom of God is at hand!

On a recent trip to South Africa, I saw the rule and reign of God—His Kingdom at hand—while we were enjoying great steak with a large group at a restaurant. The manager came over to the table to check on us and ask how our service was. As we talked with him, I felt as though I had an impression—a word of knowledge—for him (see 1 Corinthians 12:8). I felt he had pain in his shoulder. I took a risk and shared it with him. The word I shared did not apply to him at all, so I asked if he had any pain anywhere else. Nope.

Rather than being discouraged, I trusted that the Kingdom of God was at hand, even if I had missed it on a word of knowledge. "If you did have pain," I explained, "I would offer to pray for you, and I believe Jesus would take that pain away. Do any of your staff have pain?" I let the manager know that my team and I loved to pray for people, and that if he or any of his staff would like prayer before we left, we would be happy to pray for anyone who wanted it. He said he might send some people over after our meal. Honestly, I did not think he would. We all assumed we would not see him again.

A short while later, one of the ladies on our team went to use the restroom. On her way back to the table, she noticed one of the servers and thought she had a word of knowledge for her— pain in her foot. My friend had just seen me miss it on a word of knowledge, but that did not deter her. She knew that the Kingdom of God was still at hand, so she shared the word with the server and offered prayer. As she prayed, the server reported that all the pain left, and she gave her life to Jesus as a result.

What we did not realize was that the server then went to her manager and told him what she had just experienced—the same manager whom I had missed a word of knowledge with and whom we had just asked to send his employees to our table for prayer.

What happened next was an in-breaking of the Kingdom of God. As one restaurant staff person after another came to our table, we began to see healing after healing, followed by salvation after salvation. Two hours later we were still in the restaurant, still praying for staff. People were healed from various pains and sicknesses, several experienced deliverance from demons, and another man received the baptism of the Holy Spirit and the gift of tongues. Most of the servers and kitchen staff were on the floor, under the power of the presence of God. In all, fifteen people gave their lives to Jesus for the first time that night. The Kingdom of God was at hand in the steak restaurant.

Jesus' Means: The Holy Spirit

Many people disqualify themselves from the Jesus style of ministry because they think, *Well, He could do that because He was Jesus!* He was God in the flesh. He was the Word through whom all things were created. Of course He could raise a dead girl to life. Of course He could use mere words to halt a storm. Of course He could cause a blind person to see. God can do anything!

Philippians 2:6–7 says that Jesus, "though he was in the form of God, did not count equality with God a thing to be grasped, but emptied himself by taking the form of a servant, being born in the likeness of men" (ESV). Jesus never ceased being God, and yet He voluntarily suspended the independent exercise of His divine attributes so that He might live a fully human life. If Jesus did not heal the sick and raise the dead out of His own divine powers, how did He do it? Through the empowerment of the Holy Spirit.

At the scene of Jesus' baptism, we see the Holy Spirit come upon Him for the first time:

> When all the people were being baptized, Jesus was baptized too. And as he was praying, heaven was opened and the Holy Spirit descended on him in bodily form like a dove. And a voice came from heaven: "You are my Son, whom I love; with you I am well pleased."
>
> Luke 3:21–22

This beautiful Trinitarian picture shows the Father sending the Spirit to the Son.

Again we see the Spirit resting upon Jesus as He leaves the wilderness in Luke 4:14 and returns "in the power of the Spirit" to begin ministering to people. Jesus' mission statement that I discussed earlier in this chapter begins with "The Spirit of the Lord is upon me" (Luke 4:18 NKJV). Acts 10:38 tells us that "God anointed Jesus of Nazareth with the Holy Spirit and power," and that "he went around doing good and healing all who were under the power of the devil." The empowerment of the Holy Spirit was the key to Jesus' ability to walk in supernatural authority. It was by the Spirit that He healed the sick, raised the dead and cleansed the lepers. Without the gift of the Spirit from the Father, the Son could do nothing (see John 5:19–20). The Spirit empowered Jesus to put the Father on display with love and power.

The story did not end there. Jesus said something astonishing to His disciples right before He ascended into heaven: "But you will receive power when the Holy Spirit comes on you; and you will be my witnesses in Jerusalem, and in all Judea and Samaria, and to the ends of the earth" (Acts 1:8). He gave them instructions to stay in town until the Holy Spirit came on them. When the Day of Pentecost arrived, the Holy Spirit fell mightily upon the disciples and upon all Jesus' followers gathered together praying.

Not only that, but Peter boldly declared that this outpouring of the Spirit was the fulfillment of Joel's prophecy: "In the last days, God says, I will pour out my Spirit on all people" (Acts 2:17). From that moment on, we see the Church birthed in power, miracles, and signs and wonders.

The same Holy Spirit who empowered Jesus to do the work of the ministry lives in every believer. The same means by which Jesus healed the sick, cast out demons and raised the dead is alive and powerful within us. Jesus' means is our means: the Holy Spirit. Only through the Spirit's empowerment can we put Jesus on display with love and power to those around us. Without the Spirit, we have nothing to offer. But through the gift of the Spirit, God can accomplish anything through us. In fact, Jesus says we will do even greater things than He did (see John 14:12–14). Nothing is impossible with the empowerment of the Holy Spirit.

The Holy Spirit both lives *in* the believer and comes *on* the believer. We need both functions of the Spirit. His *indwelling* presence unites us to Christ and to fellow believers. He is our Helper and Counselor in times of need. He refines us deeper into the image of Christ and grows the fruit of the Spirit within us. The Holy Spirit also comes *on* us, working through us to accomplish specific tasks we could not do apart from Him. He gives spiritual gifts as He sees fit, to empower us for works of service. We need both the inner and outer workings of the Spirit to live the life God intends for us.

As I said, we have nothing to offer without the working of the Holy Spirit. I was on a conference trip with my son Tyler and a friend. We were taking a few hours out of the conference to sightsee, and we decided to visit a famous memorial site not far away. The Uber driver we hired to take us to the landmark was Yamana, a devout Muslim.

As we talked, I asked Yamana about her family and her faith. I purposely did not say anything about our being Christians or about Jesus; I just listened to her story. A little while into the conversation, I felt I had four words of knowledge about her health—stress headaches, difficulty sleeping and pain in her lower back and neck.

I asked Yamana if she had these problems. "Yes, I have all of those," she replied in shock.

I asked her, "What's your pain level on a scale of zero to ten?"

"It's a nine," she said. "How did you know these things? I've had this pain for years."

I told her I have a gift where I get pictures and impressions of what is going on in people's lives. What I did not tell her is that this gift is the Holy Spirit, who is given to every believer (see 1 Corinthians 12:4–11).

"Wow, that's very interesting," she replied.

"Yamana, would you like me to do something about those conditions and take the pain away?"

"You can do that? How?"

"Yes, I can. When you drop me off, if you give me one minute, I can take care of it." She asked me how I would take care of it, and I explained that I would just speak to her pain and tell it to go, and it would.

"Please do it," she said.

How did I know the pain would leave? I did not. But I know who Jesus is. I know He has commissioned me to heal the sick. I know that the Kingdom of God is at hand, and that means that the Kingdom is also breaking in everywhere we go, including on an Uber ride with a Muslim driver.

We continued with minor chitchat, and about three minutes later Yamana blurted out, "Did you just do that thing?"

"I haven't done anything," I told her.

"I'm hot all over my body!" she said. "Like I'm sweating. And all the pain just left my back!"

"That's very interesting," I said with a smile. Tyler and our friend were trying to hide their shock as well. "Sometimes it just leaks out of me," I said with a wink and a smile toward the back seat.

The Holy Spirit was sovereignly healing Yamana. She explained that her back pain was totally gone, her neck was very hot and the neck pain had gone down to a level four. She was bewildered.

When we arrived at the memorial, I asked her if the rest of the pain had left. "No, but I'm still hot all over," she replied.

I told her the rest of the pain would leave now. I asked if I could touch her hand, and I was surprised when she said yes, because I knew this was not something a Muslim woman would normally allow. I commanded all the remaining neck pain to leave. I prayed twice, and the second time, all the pain left.

Yamana asked me how I had done it. I explained, "The gift I have is the Holy Spirit. I'm a Christian. What you just experienced was Jesus healing you. Jesus loves you." I explained the Gospel message as simply as I could and asked, "Have you ever experienced Allah like this or received healing from Allah?"

"No," she replied.

"Well, this is what Jesus does, and I'm His follower. As Christians, this is what we do. This is the love of God expressed to you, that Jesus is pursuing a relationship with you."

Yamana said, "I believe in Allah, but I don't know how you did this."

Again I told her that Jesus was the one who did it. She was definitely perplexed and was having to rethink a lot of what she believed about Jesus. I would have loved to talk with her more, but security guards around the memorial were preventing cars from lingering. I don't know what happened to her after that, but I do know that the Holy Spirit came upon her and Jesus was glorified. Her body was healed, and she began wrestling with some real questions about what she believed and who Jesus really is.

The Holy Spirit was the means by which our driver was healed that day; she was not healed by my prayers or anything else. The

Spirit made Himself known before I even prayed or said a word about Jesus. When we partner with the empowering Holy Spirit, as Jesus did, we can have the same kinds of outcomes that Jesus had.

Power evangelism is simply learning how to rely on the Holy Spirit, not on what we can do in our own strength. We are partnering with God to do the work of God. Since it is His work, we need His presence and power to accomplish it. It is about a relationship with the Holy Spirit and relying on that relationship to empower us as we go out into the world to put Jesus on display.

Jesus' Method: Reproducible

How is it that a ragtag group of disciples thought that they could heal the sick, just as Jesus had done? What made them believe that demons would flee at their command? It is astounding, really. During the three years Jesus spent with them, not only did He perform miracles, He also infused them with the message that they could do the same. Jesus intentionally did ministry in a way that was reproducible.

At the outset of His ministry, you see one person—Jesus—operating in the power of the Kingdom. After the disciples followed Jesus for a period of time and observed Him ministering in power, He then sent them out to do the same, duplicating His own ministry. He transferred His authority to them: "When Jesus had called the Twelve together, he gave them power and authority to drive out all demons and to cure diseases, and he sent them out to proclaim the kingdom of God and to heal the sick" (Luke 9:1–2). Now twelve more people were doing the work of the ministry.

Shortly after the disciples returned, we see Jesus reproducing His ministry even further: "After this the Lord appointed seventy-two others and sent them two by two ahead of him to every town and place where he was about to go. . . . The seventy-two returned with joy and said, 'Lord, even the demons submit to us in your name'"

(Luke 10:1, 17). Now there were a total of 85 people spreading the message of the Kingdom, healing the sick and casting out demons.

After the resurrection, we see Jesus again talking with His disciples, telling them that they, too, are to reproduce His ministry:

> All authority in heaven and on earth has been given to me. Therefore go and make disciples of all nations, baptizing them in the name of the Father and of the Son and of the Holy Spirit, and teaching them to obey everything I have commanded you.
>
> Matthew 28:18–20

That means that we, too, have been commissioned to do everything Jesus commanded the disciples to do, and to reproduce His ministry. Jesus' commission to the disciples to heal the sick and proclaim the message of the Kingdom is now also our commission. Jesus' ministry was never meant to be self-contained, nor was it meant to end with the disciples. It has been reproduced disciple to disciple down to us today, and it will continue until His return.

Jesus' Model: Show-and-Tell Gospel

Jesus was known for His great teachings—the Sermon on the Mount in Matthew 5–7, the Parables of the Kingdom in Matthew 13, the Upper Room Discourse in John 13–17, to name a few. But Jesus not only told about the power of God, He showed it. Matthew summarizes Jesus' ministry this way: "Jesus went through all the towns and villages, teaching in their synagogues, proclaiming the good news of the kingdom and healing every disease and sickness" (Matthew 9:35). Jesus taught and He healed. His model was show-and-tell.

Proclamation was intimately tied with demonstration, and vice versa. The Gospel was never intended to be absent of either proclamation or demonstration. Don't be fooled into thinking some people are called or gifted only to preach the Good News and never to demonstrate the reality of that Good News, or likewise that some people are called to demonstrate it without proclaiming it. The Jesus style of the Gospel embodied both, never to be separated.

The proclamation of the Gospel delivers the transformative message of Jesus, and demonstration delivers the transformative activity of Jesus. This is the message we proclaim: *Jesus is the only way to the Father and has taken away the sins of the world.* He has empowered us with grace and made us sons of inheritance and ambassadors of His Good News. We demonstrate the reality of that Good News by healing the sick, casting out demons, loving others, feeding the poor and setting the oppressed free.

May we never buy into the lie that demonstration and proclamation are separate, or only for a gifted few. Rather, may we look to Jesus and do what He did and what He is still doing through the empowerment of the Holy Spirit given to every believer. May the world around us see, feel, know and experience the reality of the Good News with words, love and truth, coupled with the demonstrated embrace of healing the brokenhearted, setting the captive free and opening the eyes of the blind. The Gospel is total dependence on a good God who risked all for us, that we might be people who risk. The fruit of the Gospel is demonstrated and proclaimed in words coupled with power. We are to demonstrate the Gospel in all areas of our life and proclaim it by how we live and speak. Jesus' show-and-tell model is our model, too.

Jesus and Ministry Today

What do Jesus' mission, message, means, method and model have to do with us today? Just because it worked two millennia ago in Palestine, will it work in my life today? Will it work when I am getting groceries, pumping gas or on the job? I believe it does! We have been commissioned with Jesus' same mission to heal the sick and bring freedom to the captive. We have His same message of the reality of God's Kingdom breaking in right now so that God's will is done on the earth. We have the gift of the same means Jesus did—the empowerment of the Holy Spirit. His method is reproducible, so we can reproduce it, too. And we can also use Jesus' model of show-and-tell to bring both truth and freedom to the people around us.

Here is an example of what a demonstration and proclamation of the Gospel might look like. During a recent trip, I picked up my brand-new suitcase from baggage claim, and I saw that the zippers had popped off. Thankfully, none of my belongings were damaged, but the suitcase was destroyed. I had packed a small fold-up duffel bag just in case something happened, and I transferred all my belongings to the duffel. I had recently purchased the suitcase on Amazon, and I did not know how I was going to process submitting a refund request online and mailing the busted suitcase back. That was virtually impossible since I was far from home. But I did not want to bring the broken suitcase home on an airplane, so I searched for a phone number I could use to actually call someone and figure out a solution.

As I picked up the phone, I thought, *I wonder if this is going to be a divine setup.* I knew Jesus' mission was to heal the wounded and set the captives free. And I knew that the same Holy Spirit who empowered Jesus was also with me. I just did not know what that had to do with my broken luggage, but I was willing to find out.

A representative named Nicole answered my call, and I explained the situation to her. As I talked with her on the phone, again the question resonated in the back of my mind: *Does Jesus want to do something with this person while I have her on the phone?*

Nicole kept apologizing because she was coughing and clearing her throat. She said she had a cold, so I thought to myself, *I'll see if she will let me pray for her before we get off this call.* As I was thinking that, I had three impressions about issues she was having in her body in addition to her cold. During one of the waiting pauses that inevitably happen during customer service calls, I said, "Nicole, do you happen to have these three conditions? Have you been having migraine headaches, a problem in your neck down into your shoulder and an issue in your back?"

Nicole freaked out and said, "How did you know? You're weirding me out here and giving me goose bumps!"

I asked her what her pain level was on a scale from zero to ten, and she said it was a five, but if she moved a certain way, it went up to seven. Then I told her, "Sometimes I get pictures and impressions for people. I didn't know about the conditions in your body, but Jesus did, and I believe He wants to heal you. I'm going to pray for you, and all this pain is going to leave, and the cold in your chest is going to go." Then I just started praying, speaking to the pain and the pressure in her chest and telling them to leave. I told her, "You're going to feel the presence of God come through your body right now."

"Oh my gosh, I can feel that!" Nicole started freaking out again. "What's going on?" she asked me.

I asked her for an update on her pain level, and she said, "It's literally almost gone, just a little bit more." So I prayed again.

"Oh my gosh, my throat was killing me, and now the pain is completely gone!" she told me. "The pressure in my chest left, too."

I noticed that Nicole was not coughing any longer. All the pain had left her neck and back, and she kept asking with astonishment, "What's happening to me?"

I explained that Jesus was the one touching her body, and I told her, "This is what Jesus does. He heals the sick." I then said, "Nicole, let me ask you a question. If Jesus was knocking at the door of your heart, would you open it or ignore it?"

"Oh, I would open the door!"

"I think He's knocking at the door of your heart right now. Wouldn't you agree?" I asked.

"Yes!" she exclaimed.

"Would you like to give your heart to Jesus?"

"Yes, I want to give my heart to Jesus," she answered.

I prayed for her over the phone as she gave her life to the Lord. I asked God to come and touch her more with His presence. As we prayed, Nicole said she felt a warmth and presence come all through her body. "What in the world is this?" she asked.

"This is the love of Jesus," I answered. "God has come near you! You know, I think my bag breaking was a divine setup. I would give a million bags if it meant that you encountered Jesus!"

She said, "I hate to say this, but I'm glad your bag broke. You don't know how much I needed this. This last year has been so hard for me."

"Nicole, Jesus knew that," I replied. "He loves you, and He'll let my bag break so that your body can be healed and your heart will open to Him."

She was doing her best to hold back tears, and she kept exclaiming, "I can't believe this! This is so unreal! I have goose bumps all over, and I feel that heat all over, too."

The Kingdom of God is always at hand, even if your luggage gets destroyed. You never know where the Kingdom will break in. Jesus is always on mission, and the Holy Spirit is still empowering people today. All we have to do is partner with Jesus in His ministry.

The world around us is being changed as the Church becomes Jesus with skin on—not changed by our theological studies, doctrines and religious traditions alone, but changed when we also put Jesus on display with love and power. If our theological studies, doctrines and religious traditions don't reflect the 5 M's of Jesus' ministry, then we have a powerless gospel. It is the demonstration and proclamation of the Gospel combined together that change the world around us. It is an empowered and equipped Church that will change the world.

3

THE GOSPEL OF THE KINGDOM IS AT HAND

I don't get the Gospel. I don't fully understand how good God is, how lost I am without Him or how good and in right standing I now am because I have been hidden in Christ. I forget how real God is, how near He is, how far I am and yet how close I am to Him. It is scary to believe we can be so far away when He is so near, and be so close when He seems so far away. But throughout the Bible we see people who are so near, yet so far. So far, yet so near.

Jesus—God in flesh—was talking to the religious leaders of the day. They proclaimed to know God and should have been able to recognize and know Jesus as God, but they were so blinded by their own pride and understanding of the Scriptures that their ears became deaf and their hearts became hardened. They searched and studied the Scriptures but were not able to discern the Word who had become flesh and was speaking to them. They were so near, yet so far.

We see the same thing happening all the way back to the beginning of mankind, with Adam. He had known the delight of God.

But after biting into the poisonous lies of the serpent, he was so far, but so near—trying to be hidden, covering himself up with his own best efforts, trying to hide his blunderous sin. Fear gripped him, where friendship had once beckoned him. God was so near, calling out his name, but Adam was so far away, hidden by shame. He played hide while God played seek. The Gospel came shouting out his name: *"Adam, where are you?!"*

The wayward son in the prodigal story was so near to his father's heart even though he was still far off, while the older brother was so close, but so far in his heart. The adulterous woman who was caught in her sin, deserving punishment according to the Law, was so far, but so near that Jesus would step in front of the stones that were to be cast her way and say with love and truth that the man without sin should cast the first stone. The disciples who had been called by name and lived with Jesus day in and day out for three years still did not understand who their Teacher was, or what His mission or their call was. So close, yet so far.

A sick woman with a bleeding condition was hidden in the crowd, yet she was so close that in a sea of countless hands reaching out toward Him, she was able to brush against the edge of Jesus' garment as He exclaimed, "Who touched me?" Seemingly so far away, forgotten, lost in the throng, yet so close that healing power flowed out upon this sick woman lost in the crowd.

Judas was invited to be a friend and a disciple, one entrusted with so much. He was so close, but so far because of the darkness hidden in his heart. He leaned in and kissed Jesus on the cheek, only to betray Him for thirty pieces of silver. So close, yet so far.

Peter believed and proclaimed with a self-empowering boldness that he would never turn his back on Jesus. He felt so close, but was so far in his own self-confidence. He was soon schooled by the reality of his denial and hid himself away on a boat in the middle of a lake, trying to remove himself far from the pain, shame and truth of his own weakness. Then he heard the close sound of a betrayed Friend calling him to the fellowship of a meal. So far, yet so near as Jesus restored a coward into a bold proclaimer!

The examples are so many, but the message is the same: so far, yet so near; so near, yet so far. Hidden, yet sought after.

The Gospel is about God's grace, not our self-effort; His love, not our sin. It is our blindness, but His ability to open our eyes. It is the Gospel—good news to the poor in spirit and bad news to the fool in his heart who refuses to accept the wounds of a Friend and the healing of a Physician. We are not so far that we cannot come near, but we can think we are so close that we become so far.

I don't get the Gospel. It gets me!

The Kingdom Has Come Near

"Jesus went into Galilee, proclaiming the good news of God. 'The time has come,' he said. 'The kingdom of God has come near. Repent and believe the good news!'" (Mark 1:14–15).

From the very first moment of Jesus' ministry on earth, He proclaimed the message of the Kingdom of God. It was here. It was breaking into this world. It had real-life ramifications. It meant the old era had passed and a new era had been inaugurated. The coming of the Kingdom changed everything.

Those around Jesus could see that something had fundamentally changed. Something was different about this man Jesus and this Kingdom He announced. And yet, not all was right in the world, either.

John the Baptist knew this more than anyone. At the outset of Jesus' ministry, John had boldly been the first to proclaim about Him, "Behold, the Lamb of God, who takes away the sin of the world!" (John 1:29 ESV). John knew that the King and Kingdom had come, and he knew that Jesus was the Messiah sent to save the world—until John found himself in prison and began questioning everything and asking himself, *Is He the one?*

In the shadowy darkness of a prison cell, John the Baptist was alone with his darkening thoughts. Hope is hard to find in prison. His hope had been in Jesus. But if Jesus was really the Messiah, why was John in prison? When was Jesus going to save Israel and establish the Kingdom? Was John mistaken when he said this was the Lamb of God? What if it was all just overexcitement and misplaced hope?

Matthew 11:2–6 tells us what happened next:

> When John, who was in prison, heard about the deeds of the Messiah, he sent his disciples to ask him, "Are you the one who is to come, or should we expect someone else?"
>
> Jesus replied, "Go back and report to John what you hear and see: The blind receive sight, the lame walk, those who have leprosy are cleansed, the deaf hear, the dead are raised, and the good news is proclaimed to the poor. Blessed is anyone who does not stumble on account of me."

Jesus' response to John's doubts was to share the testimony of the in-breaking of the Kingdom. In its wake the blind saw. The lame walked. The leper was cleansed. The deaf heard. The dead were raised. And the poor were comforted with the Good News. This is what it looks like when the Kingdom comes.

In other words, signs and wonders authenticate the Kingdom. We know that the Kingdom has come and the Gospel has power because of something we can see, not just something we know to be true by faith. We can see healings, deliverances, and other signs and wonders, and those things authenticate Jesus and His message. Signs and wonders are not just a miracle for their recipient; they are a comfort to us all in our time of doubt and struggle. It is for all of us locked inside a prison where we question everything we thought we knew about Jesus. His Kingdom has come and is being expressed in love and power, and His will is being done.

The Good News Then and Now

The Good News then is the Good News now. The Father God sent Jesus into a world of unbelief, rebelliousness and disobedience to the Father's heart and ways. He sent His Son not to condemn the world, for the world was already condemned and made a slave to sin and death (see John 3:17). But in the darkness came a ray of light, Immanuel, God with us, who pierced and pushed back the darkness with His life, death and resurrection in order to reach the whole world with His love.

The light of His love is not turning from darkness but is penetrating right through it, aimed at destroying the lies and the grip of fear that darkness brings. Jesus came into the greatest darkness so we could embrace the light of His truth and love and see ourselves made in His image—not the image of darkness, but the image of His light.

The dark arts of unbelief, rebelliousness, disobedience, sin and death were defeated by the love and gift of a good Father displayed through Jesus. Now He sends us, the Church, into dark places to shine the light of His love and set those who are captives to darkness free by the Father's embrace. This is the Good News—we get to announce and demonstrate the finished work of the cross and embrace the world with His love.

The Kingdom has come in the person of Jesus Christ, and through Him we have life and salvation. Through Jesus we have redemption out of the kingdom of darkness and we are placed back into the Kingdom of God, where we can walk in the fullness of what He intended for us from the beginning of creation. This Good News tells us that we are no longer slaves to sin, but that we are now adopted sons of God (see Romans 8:15; Galatians 4:7). We are told in Colossians 1:13–14 that "he has rescued us from the dominion of darkness and brought us into the kingdom of the Son he loves, in whom we have redemption, the forgiveness of sins." This is the Good News!

In God's Kingdom, His rule and reign are executed. His desires are being expressed and made reality. His Kingdom is where His will is being done. When someone receives forgiveness of sin, the Kingdom has come upon that person. When the curse of sickness or death is broken over someone's life, the Kingdom has come upon him or her. God's will is being done. When a demonized person is set free, God's authority has been expressed and the Kingdom has come. When the poor are fed and the brokenhearted are comforted, the Kingdom has come.

The Gospel works! It has the power to transform a person's life. I was talking on the phone with a customer service agent about one of my accounts, and I sensed Jesus' desire for me to share the Gospel with her. She was in her sixties and had suffered joint pain for decades. I had three impressions that the Holy Spirit dropped into my heart for her. She was so stunned that I knew what was going on with her that it opened up the opportunity for me to pray for her. When I did, all her pain left!

She told me, "As soon as you asked me about those conditions, I felt a tingling and warmth all over my body! I've been struggling with faith to believe."

I realized that my nudge to share the Good News was God's idea. I told her, "Jesus is giving you the gift of faith to believe. What you experienced is Jesus. He sees you and loves you. I didn't know anything about you; I simply listened to His voice and shared with you what I felt I heard. Jesus loves you so much."

I briefly explained how Jesus had died for her so that she could join Him in His Kingdom, and that He wanted a relationship with her. Then I asked, "If Jesus was standing at the door of your heart and knocking, would you let Jesus in or ignore His knock?"

"Oh, I would invite Him in!" she said.

I said, "I believe He's knocking at the door of your heart right now. That's what you're experiencing. Just as Jesus took the pain out of your body, He also wants to take the pain out of your heart." Then I led her in a prayer over the phone as she opened her heart to Him. This lady was a customer service agent just doing her job, but God had good news for her. She had lived all her life without knowing how good the Good News was for her, until that phone call.

On another occasion, I had to take my car to a mechanic. When I came back to pick it up, I asked the man if I could pray for him. He said he had some family concerns. I also asked him if there were any problems in his body. He said he had knee problems. As I prayed for him, he said he felt a cool presence come over his knee and all the pain left.

"Do you have a relationship with Jesus?" I asked.

"I grew up knowing about prayer from my mama," he said. "But I have seen so much fighting in the Church that it made me not want to be part of it."

"Jesus is calling you into a relationship with Him," I told him as I began to share the love of God and the message of the Gospel with him. I explained how Jesus loved him and had given His life for him. Because this mechanic experienced the Gospel of the Kingdom at hand, he opened his heart to Jesus. There in his front yard, I led him to the Lord.

The Present/Future Kingdom

Jesus spoke of the Kingdom of God in a paradoxical way, as both present and future. He spoke of the Kingdom that was here and at hand, and He also spoke of the Kingdom that would come. In the life of Jesus we see the inauguration of the Kingdom, but in His Second Coming we will see the fullness of the Kingdom. In this way the Kingdom is both "now" and "not yet." Through the inauguration of the Kingdom, we see God's will being executed. As Jesus told John the Baptist, the lame were walking and the blind were seeing.

Not everyone on earth was healed, however. Not everyone is healed today. God's will is not entirely being done today, but His Kingdom is expanding. His Kingdom is here, and His Kingdom will fully come. We live in a time between two realities. Currently, we live amidst the coexistence of this present evil age and the in-breaking of the age to come. In the coming age, the will of God will fully be expressed on earth, but until then, we live in the paradoxical, mysterious tension of two Kingdom realities—now and not yet.

There have been many times when I prayed for people and nothing seemed to happen. I have prayed for people who felt sicker after I prayed, and I have prayed for people who died. When we embrace the now and not yet of the Kingdom, we can learn to live with the tension of seeing tremendous Kingdom breakthrough and tremendous pain or heartbreak at the same time.

One evening I prayed for a lady in a drive-thru window. She had been in an accident and was suffering from whiplash. I prayed a quick prayer for her, and God healed her of her pain. She was totally shocked.

What you might find more shocking is that I was on my way home from the urgent care center with one of my sons, who was running a fever and was very sick. At the time, we also had another son who had recently been hospitalized and was suffering badly from an unknown illness. Our dog had developed a bizarre hip condition and could not walk well. And I had woken up before dawn that morning to take my mom to surgery for a deviated septum, a condition I had seen God heal in others many times.

The Kingdom of God was at hand in that moment; the drive-thru lady was healed! But all these other situations in my life were showing me the paradox and tension we live in. We cannot let the not yets of our lives keep us from actively engaging in God's plan to advance His Kingdom in the now.

In the Lord's Prayer, Jesus instructed us to pray "your kingdom come, your will be done, on earth as it is in heaven" (Matthew

6:10). In heaven, God's will is perfectly manifested. There is no sickness, sin or death. All things are in alignment with the way God wants them to be. But Jesus does not want us to be content with a heaven-less earth. Rather than being discouraged that the fullness of the Kingdom has not yet come or resigning ourselves to a Kingdom-less reality, Jesus told us to pray that the Kingdom would come so that earth would be more like heaven. When we pray for His Kingdom to come on earth as it is in heaven, we are asking for the future to come into the now. We are asking for the not-yet things of the Kingdom to be expressed in the now of our daily lives.

A Defeated, Still-Fighting Enemy

We also have an enemy who has already been defeated through the cross (see Colossians 2:15), but who is still wreaking havoc until he is ultimately bound at the fullness of the Kingdom. Enemy forces at the end of World War II can serve as one analogy for the power of our defeated enemy. Even after Germany had surrendered and the war in Europe was over, individual soldiers were still holding their ground throughout France, Belgium and other parts of Europe. Allied forces had to go house to house to root out and defeat these enemies, even though the war was over and they were already defeated. Japanese soldier Hiroo Onoda continued to fight in the Philippines until 1974 for Japan—29 years after his country had been defeated and the war had ended.

In the same way, we have a defeated enemy who is still causing damage, oppressing people and trying to take over God's Kingdom. We still have sickness, emotional distress and death in this present age. Through the cross we have victory, but the fullness of that victory is yet to be manifested.

The enemy causes harm in many ways. He brings illness both in body and mind (see Mark 9:17–27; Matthew 17:14–18). He causes confusion (see 2 Corinthians 11:13–15). He opposes God's plans (see Matthew 16:21–23; 1 Thessalonians 2:17–18). He tempts us (see Matthew 6:13; Luke 4:1–13). And he accuses us (see Revelation 12:10).

First Peter 5:8–9 tells us,

> Be alert and of sober mind. Your enemy the devil prowls around like a roaring lion looking for someone to devour. Resist him, standing firm in the faith, because you know that the family of believers throughout the world is undergoing the same kind of sufferings.

During this time of the now and not yet, we need to oppose the works of the enemy diligently in order to see the Kingdom of God break through.

One way we can oppose the evil one is by actively pursuing Jesus and partnering with Him to advance the Kingdom. When we pray for the sick or comfort the oppressed, the enemy's grip is loosened on their lives and he loses ground. Every time the Kingdom of God is advanced, the kingdom of darkness suffers and is pushed back as heaven breaks in.

Satan, the crafty serpent who slithered his way into the garden, being drunk on his own self-proclaimed wisdom, sought to destroy the Kingdom of God and the authority God gave man to be fruitful, multiply and subdue the earth. The enemy deceived Adam and Eve, but the resulting curse was that while he struck the heel of mankind, mankind (through Jesus) would crush his head (see Genesis 3:14–15). The cross of Christ would overcome Satan's schemes for evil and deliver a crushing blow to his head.

Now the Church has been commissioned to plunder the enemy's kingdom. God's Kingdom is executed through the Church and the authority Jesus has entrusted to us. Jesus said in the Great Commission, "All authority in heaven and on earth has been given to me. Therefore go" (Matthew 28:18–19).

Just as we are recipients of God's Kingdom, we have also been commissioned as ambassadors of that Kingdom. God has chosen those He has rescued to, in turn, become rescuers. In His Kingdom, we are in His protection and care. But His place of protection also happens to be right in the middle of the kingdom of darkness and on the battlefield of this two-kingdom war. Following Jesus means going back into the dark places from which we were freed, to act as His ambassadors to those who are still living in darkness (see Matthew 5:14–16). We are to ravage the enemy's ranks and bring people into the Kingdom of God.

Our enemy does not take this lightly, and he often causes pushback in the life of the believer. This is to be expected and is not a sign of failure. In fact, the more we are actively advancing the Kingdom, the more we become the enemy's target. Rather than being discouraged by the pushback, we fight back by recognizing his schemes and continuing to rest in the Father's love and partner in Jesus' mission.

Living in the Tension

I have truly come to this paradoxical place where I am 100 percent shocked when I see the Kingdom come, and I am 100 percent shocked when I don't. I am still learning to live in the mystery, while at the same time pressing in for more. Living in the overlapping time of the now and not yet causes tension. We simultaneously hold two seemingly opposing truths: *The Kingdom of God has come*, and *the Kingdom of God is coming*.

What does this mean for the disciple who is learning to put Jesus on display? It means that we don't have any pat answers or religious jargon to offer people. We might not always see the Kingdom break through in the ways we expected, but we always seek to see the Kingdom advance. When we find ourselves in the tension of the now and not yet, experiencing the pushback of the enemy, we are never to let this tension keep us from pressing in for more of the Kingdom in the now.

The now expression of the Kingdom is real. There is true breakthrough available through Christ. Let us never sacrifice what God has for us in the now on the altar of what we think God is withholding for the not yet. I believe there is much more available to us in the now than what much of the Church currently operates in. This is the good news of the Gospel: Through Christ, we can experience the benefits of heaven, beginning here and now (see Ephesians 1:3).

We should never be surprised when the Kingdom comes. In Acts 3, we see the lame beggar healed by Peter and John. When the people were astonished, Peter responds with this question: "Why does this surprise you? Why do you stare at us as if by our own power or godliness we had made this man walk?" (verse 12). Peter expected the Kingdom to break through and bring healing to this lame man. He expected the impossible to be possible. He was perplexed that people were astonished at the miracle, because he knew this was what Jesus had commissioned His followers to do. Lame people walking is simply part of what happens when God's will is expressed on the earth.

I think it is clear that we should expect, not be surprised by, healings, miracles and displays of God's radical love toward us and through us. This is normal Christianity. It is His grace and goodness that heals the sick, casts out demons and brings the prodigals home.

When we approach a situation believing that God wants to break in in the now, we can be persistent in our prayers. It is easy to be discouraged when our first attempt at prayer does not seem to be answered. But a confidence in God's desire for His will to be done on earth as it is in heaven should push us toward tenacity. Like the Parable of the Widow in Luke 18:1–8, God responds to persistence. When she cried out to the judge day after day for justice on her behalf, her relentlessness was rewarded by a decisive response from the judge. "And will not God bring about justice for his chosen ones, who cry out to him day and night?" Jesus told us. "Will he keep putting them off? I tell you, he will see that they get justice, and quickly. However, when the Son of Man comes, will he find faith on the earth?" (verses 7–8).

On one of my trips, I was walking with a pastor friend of mine outside some shops when I noticed a young man walking by with a limp. Suddenly, I felt faith rise up in my heart. I knew God wanted to heal him.

"Sir, excuse me," I said. "If you let me pray for you, I believe Jesus will heal your leg."

He was stunned. "Really? You think that?" he asked skeptically.

We talked about his injury, and he said he had had it for years and he dealt with pain daily. He could not walk normally or straight with the pain in his leg. He agreed to let me pray for him.

I prayed a simple, very short prayer along the lines of "I command all the pain to go now," and I had him move his leg to see if there was any difference. No change at all. I prayed again. Still nothing. I continued praying four more times, still with no indication whatsoever of any change. By this time, the guy was looking at his watch.

"I've got to go into the store," he explained, "but I promise I'll be back in a few minutes."

Honestly, I just thought he was being polite or brushing me off. I never expected to see him again. About ten minutes later, however, I saw the man coming back out with some of his friends. I thought, *Well, this should be interesting.*

"Can you still do that thing?" he asked me. The way he said "still" made me wonder what he was thinking. I was not sure if he was serious or if he was secretly mocking me in front of his friends. Either way, I was not going to be discouraged. If he would let me pray, I would pray!

I prayed, and again nothing. I kept praying . . . and praying. Each time, I asked the young man to check his leg, and every time, there was no difference. My pastor friend was giving me the sideways "this isn't going to happen" look, but I was not deterred. As long as the man would let me pray, I would keep praying. On the 47th prayer, he was suddenly healed. All the pain vanished, and he could put weight on his leg and walk straight. Everyone was shocked. All his friends started flipping out.

The healing opened the door to be able to pray for the man and his friends for all kinds of needs. They were all so receptive after witnessing their friend being healed, and by the end, all of them had given their lives to Jesus.

My pastor friend smiled and said, "Well, I guess this puts a whole new understanding on the now and the not yet."

God had wanted the now to come for this young man. After the 5th time praying—let alone the 46th time—it would have been easy to give up and chalk up the lack of healing to the not yet. But being persistent, like the widow with the judge, changed things on the 47th time. Until we risk being foolish in the eyes of others and show a tenacity like the woman seeking justice, we will never know how much of the now can break into a not-yet moment.

The Kingdom in Community

Jesus never intended for ministry to be done in isolation. The Kingdom of God is different from the Church, but the Kingdom is never absent of the Church. The Church is made up of the people of the Kingdom. The way in which God chose to expand His Kingdom is through the Church, not only through individual Christians alone, but also through the Church together corporately.

Too many Lone Ranger Christians feel that they can put Jesus on display without honoring the way He chose to do ministry—in community. He gathered a group of disciples around Him, and they ministered together. The disciples were sent out together, and they came back together. At times, they ministered in groups of two to support each other (see Luke 10:1). At other times, we see them in threes, or with the Twelve, or in an extended group of followers of Jesus.

Too often, the pursuit of developing a lifestyle of doing Jesus-style ministry has been depicted as something you do alone with Jesus. While we all have our personal growth journey in becoming more like Jesus, the local church is the context in which healthy growth and development take place. We are not meant to embark on power evangelism single-handedly. Your ministry will always be impaired if it is not rooted in the context of the local church.

Our church, Crestwood Vineyard, began in 2013 with a group of five couples meeting in a living room. We were trying to discern God's voice and respond to His call to plant a new church in Oklahoma City. By September of that year, we had officially launched the church. From the very first moments, our church was founded on fostering a lifestyle of putting Jesus on display. We built community outreach into the fibers of our church culture.

Our first endeavors at reaching the neighborhood God sent us to were outreach events we called "Hotdogs and Healings." We would set up a grill, put up signs and start knocking door to door, offering hotdogs and prayer for anything people needed, especially healing. We saw incredible signs of God's Kingdom breaking through as people were healed and saved through these outreaches. Since then, we have tried lots of different methods and models, not only models involving how to reach our community with the Gospel, but also models for training our congregation and equipping them with the tools necessary to live a lifestyle of putting Jesus on display both through planned church outreaches and in their everyday lives.

Our church is located in the crosshairs of the gentrified arts district, the immigrant poor and public housing. We do weekly outreaches, including going door to door to talk to people and pray, going to a nearby shopping center to pray for anyone who will let us, and offering Spanish and English classes for immigrants and those trying to minister to them. Our youth group has built into its culture one youth night a month where the kids and leaders go around the city to put Jesus on display and share the Gospel through proclamation and demonstration. They gather back together after an hour to share testimonies, struggles and encouragement.

We like to say that our church is a church for the neighborhoods and the nations. The call of the Church is both local and global. The Church is always local; it has roots in a place that is home, which it reaches intentionally with the Gospel. But the Church is also global; Jesus gave us a commission to be witnesses to the ends of the earth (see Acts 1:8). At Crestwood Vineyard, not only do we take reaching our neighborhood seriously, we also value ministry to the nations. In fact, in the second Sunday service we held, the church sent me out on a trip to South Africa as its first missionary. I am so grateful that Crestwood has been the launching pad for every international trip I have taken since then. I have taken teams to minister throughout South Africa each year, equipping many believers and churches there to put Jesus on display. We have seen eight hundred people come to faith one-on-one through healings and signs and wonders, as we have demonstrated that evangelism is not just an event, but a lifestyle in the everyday places like restaurants, malls, shopping centers and out in the community. We have also taken teams into Germany and have seen several hundred people come to the Lord there as well.

Not only are churches overseas equipped and trained through these trips; these mission outreaches also give our church an opportunity to grow in power evangelism through our participation. The result goes far beyond a local community of people who partner to put Jesus on display when they are together. What we are doing fosters a lifestyle in which, even when we are away from each other, it is easy for us to put Jesus on display in our everyday lives.

When you have prayed for people with your friends during a planned outreach event and have seen God move powerfully in those situations, it becomes very easy to approach people yourself at the gas station to pray for them. Putting Jesus on display can seem intimidating on your own at first, but your faith is built through practicing in the context of a community that builds a culture of putting Jesus on display. It simply becomes a normal part of the Christian life. Evangelism is not an event; it is a lifestyle. But you have to be intentional about it, so sometimes planned events in the local church context help give us the stepping-stones that eventually lead us to a lifestyle.

The local church provides a platform in which its members can be equipped to do the ministry of Jesus. It also facilitates opportunities to practice doing ministry in a safe, relational environment where honest and constructive dialogue can be used to challenge, affirm and encourage individuals seeking to live a lifestyle of putting Jesus on display.

My wife loves to make this statement: "An equipped church is a church that can change a city." No individual alone can change a city, but a whole church equipped in knowing how to pray for the sick, cast out demons and save the lost can revolutionize an entire city, state or nation. The local church provides the context in which the Kingdom of God is expressed through nurturing, equipping, sending and celebrating the individual saint who seeks to put Jesus on display with love and power.

No Matter What

Jesus came with the message that the Kingdom of God is at hand, without any conditional statements. The Kingdom is at hand, no matter what. Often, we miss opportunities to engage in the ministry of Christ because we disqualify ourselves. We think God cannot use us because we have not prayed enough, life circumstances are hard or we are having a bad day. In fact, the opposite is true. The Kingdom works in us as it is expressed to others through us. God loves and heals us as He loves and heals others through us.

Have you ever had a bad day on purpose? The truth is, we have all had bad days on purpose. We don't have to have a bad day, but we choose to believe lies about ourselves, our situations or God that keep us in a dark place. The problem comes when we sit and fester in a bad day, and then our circumstances dictate our reality, rather than our reality (Jesus) dictating our circumstances.

I was having a bad day like that. I don't even remember what was going on that was so upsetting to me, but I know I felt as if I could not get out of it. I am growing in Christ, but the truth is that sometimes I have a bad day. My day was so bad that I remember speaking harshly to my wife, Jeanine. I yelled at my kids. I got mad at our dog, Ruby, and kicked at her. I even whacked my hand against the wall in frustration. I was making Peter look like a Sunday school saint. I was having a really bad day.

I had promised one of my sons that I would take him to a movie that night, and I took my bad attitude with me out the door. We were on the way to the theater when I got a phone call from a friend. I am not even sure why I answered my cell phone, but I did.

"Hey, Brian, how's your faith today?" this friend asked.

How's my faith today? You've got to be kidding, I thought. What kind of friend calls you up out of nowhere and asks you how your faith is? Apparently, my friends do.

"I can't talk to you right now. I'm headed to a movie with my son," I replied.

"Well, I have this guy here working on my house, and I want you to pray for him."

"What?!" I said. I couldn't believe I was hearing this. The last thing I wanted to do was pray for someone.

"Yeah, he's here trying to get some work done, but he's having trouble because his legs hurt so much. They're messed up because he has a clubfoot. He's got one leg shorter than the other, and he's in tremendous pain. You have to pray for him."

"I'm not praying for your worker. I'm headed to the movies."

My friend did not take no for an answer. "Here he is," he said.

Before I knew it, I was on the phone with this guy as I silently said some nice words in my mind about how much I needed new friends.

"Hey, I know your friend wants you to pray for me, but I don't think anything will happen," the guy said apologetically.

Yeah, I don't know if anything will happen, either, I thought to myself. *And I hate missing the previews!* But I pulled myself together enough to be cordial and talk to him.

He told me, "I've had lots of pastors, preachers and others pray for me my whole life. I've been this way since I was born, and I don't think God is going to heal me. Nothing is going to change. I just live with the pain. It's not going to work."

In my mind, I was agreeing with everything he said. Then through all that junk, I heard the Holy Spirit whisper. He was hard to hear. Not only did His direction have to filter through this man's doubts and mine, it had to filter through all the things in my bad day. It had to filter through my yelling at my wife and kids, getting angry at the dog and leaving the house in frustration as I slapped the wall. I was feeling disqualified in that moment. I figured there was no way the Holy Spirit would move through me, because I was acting outside of my identity as a follower of Christ. But the Holy Spirit was trying to remind me of who I am and how good His Good News really is.

Thankfully, I told the man I would pray. What I had in mind was that I would say a short prayer and then get off the phone right away. If we did not get into the theater in a couple of minutes, we would be late. But at least I was making progress on my attitude. I said what I thought would be a quick prayer: "Holy Spirit, would You come and stretch out his leg? Amen."

I was just about to tell him thanks for letting me pray, and then hang up, when I heard a loud scream. Bewildered, I asked, "Is that a good scream or a bad scream?"

"I don't know, man! Something's going on in my leg! I feel this pulling. Something's stretching it."

I wondered to myself, *Is this guy just pulling my leg?* (After all, I was having a bad day.) *Or is God really pulling his leg?*

"Get my friend over to see what's going on," I suggested.

"He's not here."

"Not there? Where is he?"

"He left for the store when he handed me the phone."

Seriously, I thought, *what kind of friend calls you up, asks you how your faith is, makes you pray for someone you don't want to pray for and then leaves?* Mine does.

"Is his wife there?" I asked. "Could you get her on the phone?"

She came over and they put the phone on speaker. "Brian, I don't know what to do," she said.

"That's okay. I don't know what to do, either. Let's just see what God wants to do." I told her to have him sit down and extend his legs out in front of him so they could see how much of a difference there was in their length. She said it was about a two-inch difference, and his one leg was twisted because of his condition. But he was still feeling that stretching in it.

"Just pray this with me," I instructed. She began repeating the words I prayed as she held the man's legs: "Holy Spirit, come. In Jesus' name we command the leg to grow and straighten."

Then to my shock, I heard three screams. They both screamed, and then I screamed.

My friend's wife exclaimed, "His leg just popped out! It just grew to the right length! It's completely straightened."

I could not believe what I was hearing. They were overjoyed and shouting in excitement as I hung up to walk into the movie theater, making it in right before the previews started.

A couple of minutes later, my phone rang again. It was my friend. "Brian, what did you do to my worker?"

"What do you mean? I prayed for him like you asked me to."

"Well, now I'm mad at you," he said with a smirk in his voice. "He's not getting any work done because he's walking around in circles and keeps saying, 'Oh my gosh, my leg is straight!'"

"You can't have it both ways," I said. "I'm mad at you, too!"

"Why are you mad at me?"

"Because you know how to pray for the sick. Why didn't you pray for him yourself?"

Then my friend said something profound: "Because I was having a bad day."

I learned a valuable lesson that day—the Kingdom of God is at hand, no matter what. Even when you are having a bad day on purpose. The Kingdom does not stop. God is working. God is moving.

Now, I am not advocating having a bad day on purpose. I am not advocating yelling at your wife and kids, kicking at the dog and slapping the wall. But sometimes we forget who we are. Rather than wallowing in that place of shame, we simply have to repent, change the way we think and believe the Good News. We have to remind ourselves that this is not who we are. We are righteous in Christ. We are children of God.

In that moment, the truth hit me. I felt like Peter, who had been fishing all night with no results, until Jesus came on board and worked a miracle. Suddenly, they caught so many fish that their nets were breaking. Luke 5:8 tells us, "When Simon Peter saw this, he fell at Jesus' knees and said, 'Go away from me, Lord; I am a sinful man!'" I had just been witness to a miracle, too—a man born with a clubfoot had his leg straightened and could walk straight for the first time in his life. Like Peter, I became aware of my sin. *Jesus, I sinned, but You still used me*, I thought. *You love me!* The Gospel began to do its work on my heart. I was reminded of God's great grace, the righteousness I have in Jesus, and who I am in Him, which is not based on my having a bad day on purpose.

At that point, I no longer cared about the previews or the movie, even though I had finally made it into the theater. I had just experienced the good news of the Kingdom. All I wanted to do was call home to my wife and repent. I asked her to put the other kids on the phone so I could apologize to them, too. I even asked her to put the phone up to Ruby's ear so I could repent to our dog!

I had started that evening feeling so far from God. Yet He was so near. Again, I still don't get the Gospel. It gets me every time. I don't fully understand how good God is, how lost I am without Him or how good and in right standing I now am because I have been hidden in Christ. Sometimes I forget how real God is, how near He is, how far I am, and yet how close to Him I am. It is scary to believe that we can be so far away when He is so near and so close, even when He seems so far away. But throughout the Bible, we see people who are so near, yet so far. So far, yet so near.

The Gospel of the Kingdom is truly at hand, even when you are having a bad day on purpose. I don't get the Gospel. It gets me, and it gets you—every time!

4

LIVING AN "AS YOU GO" LIFESTYLE

Putting Jesus on display with love and power is meant to be a lifestyle. But before it can become a lifestyle, you have to start somewhere. It does not matter where you start—just start!

My first introduction to Spirit-empowered ministry came in a class that Charles Bello, my mentor, friend and pastor for over twenty years, was teaching on the Kingdom of God and John Wimber's 5-step healing model. This revolutionized my understanding of what Jesus did in His ministry, how He was empowered by the Holy Spirit and how the same Spirit enables us to partner with Him in His ministry today. I finally had a solid theology for why we do ministry empowered by the Spirit, along with a practical model for how to do it. I learned that we can live a naturally supernatural lifestyle, which was both empowering and refreshing to me.

I was excited to start putting what I was learning into practice. Yet I let fear keep me from stepping out to pray for anyone during the class activation and clinic time. My first step in praying for the sick was not even with a person. It was with Snuggles the poodle, my future in-laws' family pet. Snuggles had been experiencing some sort of intestinal or stomach issue and had barely been able to walk. He had been whimpering on the couch. I knew Snuggles needed more than healing. Snuggles needed deliverance. I did not know this from some sort of supernatural insight; it was just clearly common sense because, well, he was a poodle!

Clearly, my 5-step healing model cheat sheet was not going to help me, because step 1 is the interview and I don't speak dog. So I just prayed my best prayer, hoping it would work. I picked up Snuggles and said, "Jesus, heal Snuggles. I command the pain to leave in Jesus' name."

How was I going to test it out to see if Snuggles was healed? I did not know what else to do, so I said to myself, *I hope this works*, and I held him out and dropped him to see if he was healed. And that was the day Snuggles died.

Just kidding! Snuggles ran off completely healed. And possibly traumatized. No wonder he never came around me again.

I know that sounds humorous, but it was the first experience I had of seeing someone (or something) healed when I prayed. I was ecstatic.

Charles and his wife, Dianna, continued to pour into Jeanine and me. When he would teach on power ministry somewhere, he started taking us with him to help pray for people. Eventually, he started asking us to teach the material, too. I remember being incredibly intimidated about teaching. I told Charles, "I don't even have any notes or any stories to give as illustrations."

"You can use my notes," he said. "And you can use my stories until you have stories of your own to tell."

What a gift it was, even with my knees knocking as I wondered if the Holy Spirit would anoint me the way He did Charles, or if I would look like a fool. Now, all these years later, I have too many stories and testimonies of my own to count, all because Charles shared his stories and notes, took me all over the world ministering with him and put me into situations where I would have to learn to risk so I could believe that the Holy Spirit would anoint me, as He did Charles. I would not be where I am today without this man. This is what true discipleship looks like—freely giving to another what God has given you and empowering that person to go further than you have gone.

Another huge resource I relied on was a shelf full of VHS tapes and cassette tapes someone gave me of teachings from John Wimber and from Blaine Cook (who now, many years later, has become a friend of mine). I used to spend hours and hours studying John and Blaine's teachings on the theology of the Kingdom of God, how to pray for the sick and power evangelism. Blaine became one of my biggest heroes, and I wanted to be like him. He was a businessman whom God used regularly in power evangelism, and he had amazing testimonies just from his daily life of people coming to faith all the time.

When I first learned about power ministry, I became proficient and comfortable praying for people and getting words of knowledge for healing in the Church. But I had not yet seen it happen outside the Church's four walls. I remember praying, *It's really good that it happens in here, but I've got to see it happen out there. Jesus, show me how to bring Your power to people outside the Church. Jesus, would You put on me what You put on Blaine Cook and John Wimber?*

In 1999, I heard that Blaine Cook would be teaching at a conference in Chicago. I thought just maybe if I went to this conference, I would be activated into power evangelism. I thought if God could anoint Blaine to do that stuff, just maybe God would anoint me to do the same thing. So I drove with two friends twelve hours up to Chicago. During the entire drive, I kept praying over and over for God to anoint and empower me: *God, please use me in power evangelism! I need an impartation to see the lost saved outside the Church. . . .*

During one of the conference sessions we attended, Blaine paused what he was saying and said, "You, young man. Stand up." I realized that he was pointing to me. I stood as Blaine said to me, "The Lord is anointing you for power evangelism. You are going to be used greatly in it."

It was such a surreal moment. I was blown away that God had heard the cry of my heart. (Really, it was God's heart for me. I just did not understand that at the time.) As Blaine said those words, it was as though a surge of electric power coursed through my body. With no one touching me, I shook so violently. It was the raw power of God anointing me, and it threw me backward several feet. I took out about eight rows of chairs and landed on my back, shaking as waves of electric power coursed through me.

It was a powerful impartation. As I lay there at the conference, I thanked God for our encounter. *God, You heard my prayer. You gave me the impartation I asked for in power evangelism. Now, just give me an opportunity!*

That opportunity came later that same day, when my friends and I stopped for lunch at a Popeyes Chicken restaurant. I noticed a lady standing in line, and I immediately began to feel pain shoot into one of my arms. I had a lot of experience with getting words of knowledge in the Church, and I knew that this feeling of someone else's pain is one of the ways God speaks. I felt that God wanted to heal this woman, and He was inviting me to pray for her.

Now, you would think I would be full of faith. After all, I had driven twelve hours while praying for God to meet me and empower me in power evangelism. When I got to the conference, a hero of mine in the faith had called me out of the meeting and had spoken a powerful word of impartation over me. The power of God had poured into me, and I had lain on the floor, crying out for an opportunity to put Jesus on display outside the Church.

I was in my moment of invitation and opportunity, and I was chickening out. I did not want to do it. There was no way I was going to go pray for that woman. The truth was, I became the biggest chicken that day in Popeyes Chicken!

My friend could tell something was going on. "What's happening?" he asked.

"I think God wants to heal that woman over there with a condition in her arm."

"Well, go over there!" he said. "What are you waiting for? This is what you wanted."

"No way," I said. "I'm not doing that. What if I'm wrong? What if it's just my imagination?"

"Well, if you're not going to go talk to her, I will."

"Fine, as long as you don't tell her the impression came from me," I replied, still terrified of approaching anyone or praying for people in public.

What I love about this friend is that he was not the one who got the word of knowledge that day. He was not the one whom Blaine had called out in a meeting to receive an impartation. He was not even the one who had been crying out to God, asking to be used in power evangelism. But he was the one who had the boldness to go speak to the woman! He just knew that God had given an invitation, and he wanted to respond to it. He walked up to the woman and asked her if she was experiencing pain in one of her arms.

"Yes. How did you know?" she asked.

"You see that guy over there?" my friend said with a smile as he pointed at me. God and good friends never let you get away with anything. "He felt as though God showed him that you have pain in your arm, and I believe God wants to heal it."

He went on to pray for the woman, and her arm was completely healed right there in line at Popeyes Chicken.

I learned a valuable lesson that day—that the Kingdom of God is at hand even when we are chickens, and that doing the works of Jesus is not just for the specially anointed, but for any believer who will simply believe and take a risk.

It does not matter if you get called out in a meeting and have an empowered encounter if you don't do anything with it. God has already commissioned and empowered you, and we are all responsible for taking what we have been given and doing something with it.

God had given me the impartation and the invitation, but I let fear rob me of that encounter. I learned from that experience. I learned that God is faithful to give us lots of opportunities to develop a lifestyle of putting Jesus on display with love and power. This is how I started in power evangelism—as a big chicken! And I am still finding and plucking out chicken feathers.

The Matthew 10:7-8 Lifestyle

I have only experienced angelic activity a handful of times in my life. We see that angels are very active throughout Scripture. Angels appeared to Abraham and Sarah to tell them they would have a son (see Genesis 18). An angel encouraged Gideon when he was ready to give up (see Judges 6). An angel brought food and water to Elijah so he could continue his journey (see 1 Kings 19). The angel Gabriel came to Mary to tell her she would bear the Messiah, and an angel announced to the shepherds that Jesus had been born (see Luke 1–2). Through both the Old and New Testaments, we see angels as God's messengers who worship God and do His will on earth.

One angelic encounter I did have was during a conference at the Vineyard church we were part of in 2004. The presence of God was thick in the room. As a friend of mine was speaking, out of my peripheral vision I saw a bright light rush from behind me and shoot toward the emergency exit door to the right side of the stage. As soon as I saw the light hit the door, the door flew open violently. That door was heavy and rusty; you had to really put your back into it to pry it open. There was no way that the door would spontaneously open on its own, let alone fly open. Yet the entire roomful of people saw the door fling open. A prophetic friend of mine sitting next to me leaned over and said, "Did you see that angel?"

"You mean the light? I saw a light fly to the door and open it."

"Yes. That was an angel," he said.

Suddenly, I knew exactly what message that messenger had been sent to deliver: It is time to get out of the sanctuary and into the streets. He had literally flung open the church door to make the point clear that it is time for the Church to exit the building!

You may be wondering, *I didn't have an angel tell me to get out of the sanctuary and into the streets. How do I know that's for me, too?*

I know it because you have an even better messenger. You have Jesus' words in Matthew 10:7–8. Matthew 9 portrays a beautiful montage that shows scene after scene of Jesus operating in miraculous power. Jesus healed a paralyzed man and the woman with the issue of blood. He raised a young girl from death back to life. He set the blind and the mute free. Jesus was constantly healing and touching people, liberating them from oppression. But we see a shift at the end of chapter 9. He tells His disciples that the harvest is plentiful, but the laborers are few. He is praying for God to send more workers into the harvest field.

Jesus knew that the in-breaking of the Kingdom would involve more than His ministering to people by Himself, so in Matthew 10:7–8 we see Him commissioning His disciples to do the same ministry He has been doing. He sends them out with these instructions: "As you go, proclaim this message: 'The kingdom of heaven has come near.' Heal the sick, raise the dead, cleanse those who have leprosy, drive out demons. Freely you have received; freely give." Jesus is instructing them to go out into life to demonstrate and proclaim the Kingdom of God *as they go*.

You and I have been given the same commission. We are to proclaim the message of the Kingdom, heal the sick, raise the dead, cleanse those who have leprosy and drive out demons. We see the sick around us every day—people suffering from chronic illness, acute pain, arthritis and headaches. We also encounter people tormented by emotional pain from loss, abuse, suffering and abandonment. People in need of healing cross our paths all the time. We have the power of Jesus to heal them.

Jesus also said to raise the dead. People often take this passage figuratively, and it is true that we have been commissioned to bring the spiritually dead to life with Christ. But when Jesus raised the dead, He actually brought dead corpses back to life and wellness. I have never experienced the dead being raised, but I believe we have all been commissioned by Jesus and empowered by the Spirit to do so. I have prayed for people who have died, but I have yet to see that prayer answered.

Jesus also commissioned the disciples (and us) to cleanse those who have leprosy. This may sound redundant since He had already told the disciples to heal the sick. But leprosy involved much more than physical illness. The leprous victims were ceremonially unclean and were therefore forbidden to interact with others in society or join in worship at the Temple. The command to cleanse the lepers involves bringing those who are social outcasts back into society, love, acceptance and Church family.

We are also commanded to drive out demons. Much of Jesus' ministry was marked by demons fleeing and the oppressed being set free. I believe many of the physical healings we see are simply demonic spirits of affliction or infirmity leaving people as Jesus sets them free. Jesus tells us in Luke 11:20, "But if I drive out demons by the finger of God, then the kingdom of God has come upon you." Part of the advancement of the Kingdom involves the driving out of demons.

Jesus told His disciples, along with us, to do all these things "as you go." As you go where? Wherever it is you go! We all go places every day. I go to the movies, business meetings, kids' soccer games, Walmart, Starbucks, grocery stores, fast-food drive-thrus, restaurants and all the ordinary places you go on a daily basis. We have been commissioned to bring the good news of the Gospel into those ordinary places. It is not just for mission trips or as we go to church. Mission starts when you wake up in the morning each and every day. You have become light to the world. You have come to shift the atmosphere. You have come to bring the Kingdom of God. We step out the door to put Jesus on display with love and power everywhere we go. It is not us on display; it is Him on display in us. It is submitting to that reality and saying, *Jesus, have Your way.*

"As You Go" to the Mall

I was headed into the mall one day, incredibly excited to be picking up my new MacBook Pro from the Apple Store where a couple of my friends work. I had just gotten the notification that my computer was ready for pickup, and nothing was going to stop me—or so I thought.

As I was coming around the corner, within sight of the Apple Store, another sight caught my eye: a man on crutches coming out of one of the stores. As soon as I saw him, compassion hit my heart, and I felt drawn to go pray for him. I have to admit, I just wanted to get into the Apple Store, and I had that feeling that I did not want to face the rejection of nothing happening if I prayed for him. All I wanted to do was get home and nerd out on my new MacBook Pro. I asked God, *Can it wait?*

I heard the Lord whisper back to my heart, *Yeah, it can wait.* But I knew what He was saying. It could wait, but I would be missing out on putting Jesus on display, and missing an opportunity for someone to be set free. I had a choice in the matter, but God was inviting me to join what He was doing in that moment. I knew the MacBook Pro was not going anywhere, but this man was leaving the mall and this was probably my only chance to approach him.

I walked up to the guy and simply asked what had happened to his leg. He told me that he had been in a major accident and had broken his leg and hip. He explained that after getting out of the hospital, he had been in a wheelchair for a few months and had just moved on to crutches. He suffered constant pain and could not stand or walk without the crutches, but even doing that was excruciatingly painful. His friend next to him nodded in agreement.

"I'm a Christian, a follower of Jesus, and I would love to pray for you. Would that be okay?" I asked.

"Yeah, sure you can," he said. He was open to prayer, but I could tell he was surprised that I had offered. I asked him where his pain level was on a scale from zero to ten. He said, "At the moment, it's a five."

As I began to pray for him, he exclaimed, "Oh my gosh!"

"What's going on?" I asked.

"There's a warm, tingling feeling coming all through my body!" he told me.

I continued praying, and then I asked, "Do you feel comfortable trying to do something you couldn't do before?"

He tried taking his weight off the crutches and standing on both legs. He looked in astonishment at his friend and said, "There's no more pain! This is the first time I've been able to stand upright!" His friend confirmed it, also amazed.

I asked if he wanted to try walking, and he said yes. I took his hand and his crutches and said, "Come walk with me."

As we walked up and down the mall, with me just steadying him with one hand, he slowly began to grow in confidence as the healing gradually increased. What was comical to me was that we kept walking back and forth past the Apple Store, where people

76

were staring at us with bugged eyes and gaping mouths, pointing and whispering to each other as we walked by with me holding his crutches. My friend who works there was casually explaining to people in the store that Jesus was healing someone. It opened up an opportunity for him to share Jesus with his customers and co-workers who witnessed the healing.

The man was overwhelmed, as he was walking on his own for the first time in months. He kept saying, "Is this a dream?"

"No, it's not a dream," I told him. "It's Jesus. This is what Jesus does." I then suggested, "Why don't you try walking up the stairs by yourself?"

He did it with no help from the crutches or from me. When he got to the top, he broke down crying. I held him in a tight embrace and told him how much Jesus loved him. I could tell there was more behind his tears than just his leg being healed. Jesus was radically touching this man's heart in a way he would never forget. It was beautiful.

I was just headed to the Apple Store—not doing ministry or outreach, just going about my day. Remember, it is "as you go." We are simply to respond to the Holy Spirit and put Jesus on display as we go about our everyday lives. We are all given the gift of the Holy Spirit and the commission to go in Matthew 10:7–8, and we are all called to live a lifestyle of putting Jesus on display.

"As You Go" through a Drive-Thru

Once we realize that we have been commissioned to put Jesus on display everywhere we go as we go about our ordinary day, we can begin to see God break into the mundane areas of our lives. We don't have to go on a mission trip to see the power of God break in to bring people to salvation. We don't have to go on a planned outreach with our church to see people healed. All those things are important and necessary, but we must remember that the mission is also in the mundane. The mission of God is still enacted as we go about our everyday activities. Jesus is there when we are at work, when we are playing with our kids or when we are doing necessary things like filling our car with gas or picking up milk from the store.

With six kids and busy schedules, fast-food drive-thrus are an inevitable part of our weekly routine, and a part I had started to dread. One day as I was waiting in yet another fast-food drive-thru line, I felt the Lord whisper to my heart that this could be an opportunity for a Kingdom encounter.

Really? I thought. *You've only got like fifteen seconds max with someone in a drive-thru. Is that even possible?*

But I tried it out. Since then, I have been hooked! I pray for people in drive-thrus as often as I can. For example, one day I was riding home with my friend when my wife, Jeanine, texted me to ask if we could pick up some burgers on our way home. As we drove up to the window to pay, I was in the passenger seat. I felt as though I had an impression about two conditions in the drive-thru worker's body. I asked the woman if she happened to have a problem with her wrist and shoulder.

"No," she replied, "but I have a problem in my knee from a sports injury."

In the few seconds I had at the window, I asked her what her pain level was on a scale from zero to ten. She said it was a seven, so I prayed a quick, simple prayer of command. I told her she would feel a warm presence come over her body and the pain would go. I asked her to try it out. (Keep in mind that all of this took less than twenty seconds.)

She looked at me and said, "Would you think I was crazy if I told you it worked?"

My friend and I just laughed and said no. Then I asked her to tell me what she felt.

"I felt that warm presence come into my hip, down into my knee, and all the pain left!"

I told her this was Jesus' love for her. Excited, she said, "I'll never forget this. Thank you so much!"

You know the Kingdom of God has come when the drive-thru window worker raises her hands and shouts out a "Woot! Woot!" as you drive off.

I have seen lots of people get healed in drive-thrus, and the fun part is that you often get to see them again when you go back to the same place. I have even missed it on a word of knowledge in a drive-thru before, but when I came back another time, the same worker got healed. Something that had become a mundane drudgery in my life has now become an invitation to adventures with Jesus.

"As You Go" through a Stoplight

If you think a drive-thru is fast, try praying for people at a stop-light! Jeanine and I had just left a church service when we pulled up to a red light. I was in the passenger seat with the window down, and a car pulled up next to me at the light. There was a man driving with a woman passenger, and his window was down.

I had a quick, fleeting impression, so I blurted out, "Hey! You have a problem in your mid- to lower back. Is that right?" He looked at me a little confused, so I repeated it again and pointed on my back, exactly where the pain was.

He said yes, and the woman was nodding and smiling.

I said, "Well, today the Lord Jesus heals you." Then this came rushing out of my mouth: "The depression that has hovered over your family is broken today."

The man just looked at me with that deer-in-the-headlights look, and the woman sitting in the passenger seat smiled and nod-ded her head in agreement. She reached her hand out the window with a big thumbs-up! The light turned green and we both drove on our way. The Kingdom of God is always at hand as you go, even going through a stoplight!

"As You Go" to Court

I hate to admit that I got a speeding ticket, but I did. I was ticketed for driving more than ten miles per hour over the limit, so I decided to go to court to see if the fine could be reduced so it would not affect my insurance. While I was waiting in the packed courtroom, I sat between two people on the back row. As I sat there, I was feeling embarrassed about my speeding ticket and was just trying to keep to myself. Then I felt the Holy Spirit say this was an opportunity to share the Kingdom, and I had an impression about a leg and spine issue.

In just a few minutes the judge was supposed to come in, and I knew I had to make a decision either to follow the leading of the Holy Spirit right away or just keep to myself and sit in my shame and embarrassment. It looked as if the person to my left did not want to be bothered, so I looked over at the person to my right, who I noticed had crutches leaning up against the wall. I thought I would just go for it, so I asked, "Hey, what happened to you?"

"I broke my ankle in a work accident," the person said. "It has pins inserted in it."

My immediate thought was, *I had a picture about leg and spine problems, not a broken ankle.* But since I had already engaged someone in conversation, I was going to keep going for it. I asked about the pain and was told it was constant and terrible.

I said, "I'm in here because I was speeding, but I'm a follower of Jesus. Can I pray for you?" And then I thought, *Oh, great! You look like a great follower of Jesus, sitting in court because you were speeding.* But the person did want prayer, so there in the courtroom,

I quietly spoke to the pain and told it to go. "Try moving your foot," I said.

I asked what it felt like and was told the pain had cut in half, so I asked if I could pray again. Then I added, "You'll feel a warmth and tingling go down your leg, and all the pain will leave." I quietly spoke to the pain again.

When I asked this person to check again, the response was, "There's no more pain. It's all gone! And I felt that warmth and tingling you were talking about, too."

"Have you ever felt anything like that before?"

"Never."

"Hey, this was the love of Jesus for you."

About that time, a different person sat to my left. As soon as he sat down, I knew he was the guy with the leg and spine problems the Holy Spirit had spoken to me about. I was not sure where to begin with the small talk. I said, "Man, it's a packed courtroom today."

He commented that he had been there several hours already, so I began to wonder how long this embarrassing situation would take for me. We were minutes from the judge's entrance, so I said, "You have lots of leg and spine problems, don't you?"

"Yeah." He sighed.

We introduced ourselves. I said, "See this person next to me, who had such a painful broken ankle? I prayed and all the pain left. Can I pray for you?"

"Yes!" he replied with excitement.

I quietly spoke to his spine, commanding the pain to leave. Then I asked, "Are you feeling any more pain in your spine?"

"No, it just went numb!"

The judge came in right then, and guess who he called first out of a packed courtroom—me! I approached the bench as he said, "How do you plead?"

"I'm guilty," I replied.

He looked at me and said, "This is a minor traffic offense. I'll reduce your fine. You're free to go."

The Kingdom of God is at hand, even when you are sitting in a packed courtroom, guilty of going 51 mph in a 40 mph zone.

"As You Go" in an Uber Ride

Uber is my favorite means of transportation when I don't have my own vehicle. Not only is it usually a good driving experience, but you also have an opportunity to put Jesus on display with someone you would never otherwise have a chance to interact with. As an Uber driver was driving me around one afternoon, I asked him if he had any pain in his body. I did not have any word of knowledge, nor did I notice any problems. I was just looking for a way to engage in a spiritual conversation.

This driver was surprised by my question, because he had been experiencing major discomfort in his side for months. It had been constant. He said that right before he picked me up, he had asked God to take away the discomfort.

"I think the Lord is going to answer that prayer," I told him.

"I sure hope so," he said in desperation. When we arrived at my destination, I prayed for the pain to leave his side.

"This is a miracle!" he said. "I'm searching for the pain, and it's really not there," he told me as he pushed on his side. "It's not just in my mind, Brian. Whenever I did this before, I felt terrible pain. I would have been feeling pain just sitting here this long, and I don't feel anything. God is good!" he said in astonishment.

I asked him what he had felt when I prayed for him. "I felt a presence," he answered. "Then I realized the pain was gone."

I exchanged contact information with him so we could keep in touch. That evening, he texted me to thank me and let me know he was still feeling well, with no problems. He was still amazed. He had called his mom in the Caribbean to let her know what had happened to him. He asked me if I would be willing to call her via WhatsApp on video chat to pray for her as well. We made arrangements for a call.

This man's mom had been in pain for over a year, from her hips to her feet. She did not know what was going on, and doctors did not have a diagnosis or any way to treat the pain. The only relief she would get was by taking several pain pills, but that would only help for a couple of hours. Then the intense pain would return. I prayed for her over the phone for twenty to thirty minutes. She started out in severe pain, and each time I prayed she kept feeling warmth and the pain kept decreasing. At the very end, she felt only a tinge of discomfort.

This woman's voice from so far away was filled with excitement as she thanked Jesus for His answer to prayer. As I was praying for her, she also started to walk straight instead of being hunched over. She kept saying, "Brian, I'm walking straight! I'm standing straight!" She was completely amazed by having a whole year of pain and discomfort gone.

I asked her to call me back the next morning to let me know how she was doing. She sent me a text saying she woke up feeling great. She said she slept through the night, and she had not slept like that in a year. She had always moaned and groaned through the night because of the pain, but she did not experience any of that. She still felt a little tiny bit of tingling, but that was all. She got out of bed with complete ease, walking straight and normal, with no pain. Two people experienced God's goodness, healing and presence as I simply took an Uber drive and responded to Jesus' activity.

"As You Go" to the Grocery Store

I went to a grocery store one time with my friend Mark Goering and another young man. We were looking to put Jesus on display, and we saw a lady walking with a cane. As we approached, I asked her about it. She and her husband motioned that they did not speak English, but we noticed that the clerk working at a display counter spoke Spanish. I did my best to communicate to the couple to follow us, and they did.

We walked over and asked the display clerk if she would help us translate. She was happy to, and she found out for us what had happened to the lady with the cane and what her pain level was on a scale from zero to ten. Then I asked her to help me translate a prayer.

As we prayed, the lady with the cane began to feel heat and tingling come all over her body. She became emotional and said the pain left. The clerk was shocked and said, "This is freaking me out. I feel goose bumps all over my body."

I told the clerk, "Ask her if she feels comfortable handing me the cane, taking my hand and walking up and down the grocery aisle."

The lady agreed and we were off, walking up and down the aisle. Then I let go of her hand. I had her cane in mine, and she walked perfectly up and down a couple of times with no pain and no cane, as if she had never been injured. The clerk was as overjoyed as the couple, and they all were in tears. Through the clerk, I told the healed lady this was the love of Jesus for her.

She told me in return that because of a family tragedy, she had stopped believing in God until now. I looked her right in the eye, smiled and told her how much God loved her. She was teary-eyed and so thankful. After it was all over, we asked the clerk if she had ever seen anything like this before, and she said only on TV. I smiled and said, "Well, it just happened in your store! This is what every Christian is called to do."

Four weeks later, I got a completely unexpected phone call. It was from an international number I did not recognize, so I let it go to voicemail. "Hello," the recording said. "I'm calling from Mexico. You prayed for my cousin with pain in her leg at the grocery store, and she experienced a miracle. Now she can walk without a cane. I need prayer, too. Please call me."

I called the woman back, and she told me that her cousin was still totally healed and that she no longer had pain in her legs and no longer needed a cane. I had given the lady with the cane my number, and she in turn told this cousin in Mexico about what God had done.

"It's a miracle, what happened to my cousin," this international caller exclaimed. "She gave me your number because I'm going blind in one eye. I need prayer." She explained that she only had about 10 percent of her vision left.

I prayed with her over the phone for about fifteen minutes, and during that time her eyesight improved to about 80 percent.

"It's not a miracle yet; it's still blurry. But I can see!" she exclaimed.

I was reminded of the story of when Jesus prayed for the blind man and then asked him, "Do you see anything?" The man replied, "I see people; they look like trees walking around" (Mark 8:23–24). Jesus prayed again, and the blind man could totally see. If Jesus had to pray twice, then I think we get at least a few extra tries. This lady was so grateful that her sight had improved to almost 80 percent. She said excitedly, "I can see! Even though it's blurry, I can see!" She would have let me pray longer, but she realized she had to leave for work.

I kept telling her, "This is Jesus! He loves you so much." The entire encounter was a complete surprise. I had gone out intentionally to do outreach with some friends four weeks earlier, and then God had opened an opportunity for a woman in Mexico to receive at least the beginning of healing for an eye that was going blind.

"As You Go" with Kids

From the time my kids were very young, they have grown up praying for people. Through their own hands, all six of my children have participated in healings, prophetic words, and signs and wonders, and they have seen people open their hearts to Jesus as a result. Not only have I intentionally included them whenever I am doing "as you go" ministry, I have also purposefully included them in planned outreaches. Children have incredible faith, and often people respond well to Jesus ministering through the hands of a child.

One of the things my kids have enjoyed doing is going by McDonald's and buying a huge sack of hamburgers to hand out to people. I was with my two younger daughters, Amberlyn and Ashley, passing out hamburgers one afternoon and offering to pray for people. We decided to walk into a Laundromat to see if anyone inside was hungry and wanted prayer. We met a young woman who gladly accepted a burger from my girls and let us pray for her painful back. Her back was healed, and she experienced the love and presence of God.

This woman was so touched by what God had done for her through my girls that she brought her husband to our church with her the next Sunday. The power of God met them so strongly. A few weeks later, her husband was radically saved and baptized at our church, and the woman recommitted her life to Jesus. Within the next few years, we saw them completely transformed. They went to our ministry school, were incredibly involved in our church, led small groups and outreaches and were powerful witnesses who put Jesus on display everywhere they went. All because two girls offered the woman a hamburger and prayed for her.

On another occasion, I was driving home very late one Friday night with my oldest daughter, Annalisa, who was then twelve. We drove past some gangbanger kids hanging out at the side of the road. A moment later Annalisa said, "Daddy, turn around! We need to go pray for those dudes. One of them has something wrong with his right shoulder."

I have to admit, I was a little shocked by her boldness and assurance, and I was tired and wanted to go home. Nonetheless, I turned around, and we headed back toward where we had seen the guys. They had gone into a gas station, so we pulled up as they were coming out. Meanwhile, another car pulled up, full of more gangbangers. Still in our car, I shouted out to the guys we saw, "Hey, which one of you has a problem with your right shoulder?"

This big guy walked up to the car and said, "Why? Do you guys pray for people?"

That was not the response I expected! As we got out, I replied that we did pray for people.

The guy turned to his friends and explained, "This has happened to me before." He was eager to receive prayer. He told us his right shoulder was not bothering him at that moment, but he did have trouble with it.

I began to prophesy over him, and he was just soaking it in. Then my little Annalisa became even more emboldened, pointing to each of the guys around us, looking eye to eye and saying with extreme passion and tears in her eyes, "Do you really know how much Jesus loves you?"

I should note that we are an urban church right smack-dab in the middle of a rough neighborhood. I teach my kids not to be afraid, but also to be wise and stay aware of our surroundings. I would never advocate that people carelessly take their kids into danger for danger's sake while putting Jesus on display, but we have everyone from the down-and-out to convicts to the homeless to CEOs in our congregation. And while I do not put my kids in harm's way on purpose, I have seen that those whom we often consider "dangerous" are just other people who are different from us and who have desperate needs. You have to hear from the Lord on that for yourself in these situations, and let the Holy Spirit guide and direct your interactions.

That evening, my little twelve-year-old's words were penetrating right into these tough-looking gangbangers' hearts. I could see their countenances soften, taking in what she was saying. You could feel God's presence hovering in the parking lot.

As she was doing this, I felt a pain shoot into my back, and I knew it was a word of knowledge for one of the guys in the other car that had pulled in behind me. "Which one of you has problems in your back?" I asked.

I saw a thin stream of smoke billowing out of the car, and it had a distinct smell I recognized from my past. It definitely was not a glory cloud. But the glory of God was about to invade.

The two in the front seat were playing it cool, but the guy who was toking in the back spoke up. "It's me, man!"

I asked him where his pain was, and he said in his back, right shoulder and tooth. I asked, "Will you let me pray for you? I guarantee you will be healed." I know this was a bold statement—it was just a gift of faith. He said yes, I could pray, so I grabbed the other gangbanger guy that Annalisa and I had prayed for and said, "Hey, Bro, come help me. Let's see this guy get healed."

Annalisa, the healed gangbanger and I reached our hands into the car, and we prayed a quick prayer: "Pain, go now. Get out of his body."

I looked at the guy, and he looked at his friends. He was so whacked-out! His eyes got big as he said the pain was leaving. The guys in the car were getting a little freaked out, too, having a twelve-year-old girl, a chubby white guy and a big ole gangbanger reaching into their car to pray for their friend.

The guy we prayed for just kept looking wide-eyed, as if to ask what had just happened. I said, "Bro, Jesus loves you so much!" Once again, you could see the words penetrating into his heart. I guarantee this was a night these guys would never forget. Jesus was marking each of them with a powerful encounter of His love. The entire encounter had opened up because my twelve-year-old daughter responded to a prompting of the Holy Spirit with a word of knowledge.

On another occasion, my two younger boys, Josiah and Nathaniel, had some money left over from their Christmas gifts, and

I asked them what they wanted to do with it. The boys were five years old at the time, and they said they wanted Ben 10 action-figure toys from their favorite cartoon show.

"Boys," I said, "you've got six dollars. I don't think that's enough to buy any Ben 10 toys."

They would not be dissuaded. "Please, Daddy, please! Take us to the store to get Ben 10 toys."

So being the good dad that I am, I headed to a local store with the boys, already rehearsing the financial advisement speech I would deliver to teach them that sometimes it is best to save up our money for things we really want. We arrived and started searching the toy section, with no luck. I just happened to see an employee down one of the aisles, so I asked her if they had any toys for six bucks.

"I'm not sure," she said, "but let's look." She was so sweet. She kept taking us down each aisle, looking for toys that cost $6 or under. Nothing.

Then she took us to the clearance toy section, and there were some toys under $6, but nothing the boys wanted. All they wanted was Ben 10. The lady patiently showed us the way down one more aisle, and guess what! There were some cool Ben 10 toys on sale for $4.50! The boys were excited about that and even had enough money left over to get a snake and a slinky, too.

This lady was extremely patient while serving us, so I wanted to bless her. I asked the Lord if He had something for her. The Holy Spirit began to whisper to my heart about four health conditions she had in her body. So I asked her about them, naming them specifically.

She turned to me in shock and asked, "How did you know all of that?"

"One is in your leg, isn't it?" I asked further. I did not know this piece of information at first. It came after I was faithful in sharing the part I had to begin with. The lady freaked out, again asking how I knew. "Sometimes Jesus gives me information about what's going on in people's lives because He wants to heal them, love on them and make Himself known," I explained.

"Wow, that's crazy!" she said.

"Hey, can my boys pray for you?" I asked. Not only did I know that five-year-old boys are hard to say no to, but I also doubted this lady knew how much power five-year-olds can pack when they pray. She said sure, the boys could pray.

The boys put down their toys and began to pray. I guided them along by telling them what words to pray for her body. Then I asked her what was going on in her.

"I feel better!" she said.

I asked her if all the pain in her body was gone. "Tell me the truth," I said. "You won't hurt the kids' feelings, or mine."

"I do feel better," she said, "but a couple of spots still hurt."

"Not a problem," I said. "Let me see your hand." Then we prayed again. I could feel power flowing into her as she started to lose her balance. She started laughing and freaking out. I knew these were indications of the presence of God upon her. I said, "Move your leg."

Then she really started to freak out. "There's no more pain!" She had been in pain for months, after a bad fall. She told me on a scale from zero to ten, the pain had been a level nine all the time, and it often made her cry. Surprised now, she kept saying, "I can't wait until I get home to tell my fiancé what happened!"

I asked her, "You know why this happened?"

"No. Why?"

"Because God just wanted to show you that He loves you so much." She laughed in joyous surprise.

The mission of Jesus is the same everywhere we go, and no one is ever too young or too old to partner with Jesus in putting Him on display with love and power. Children are full of faith and love, and people can feel that when children pray for them. When children share prophetic pictures or impressions for people, they are often incredibly accurate and are delivered in a way that people can receive well. God flows powerfully through children.

Freely You Have Received, Freely Give

All of us who have come to know the goodness and love of God have been given something priceless: Jesus Himself. The overflow of a thankful heart that has been touched by God should compel us to help others receive the same gift we have been given. Experience with God does not end with what God has done for us. It has feet to it. It looks like something. It looks like helping others encounter the same Jesus we have encountered. Freely we have received. Now we can also freely give away.

It is as simple as that. We don't have to have a degree in theology. We don't have to go through ministry school. All we have to do to live the Matthew 10 lifestyle is be one of the recipients of that same grace. There are no other qualifiers. It does not matter how old or young you are, how educated you are or what obstacles you have faced in life. All of us have been commissioned into the Matthew 10 lifestyle—as you go, proclaim the message of the Kingdom, heal the sick, raise the dead, cleanse the lepers and drive out demons. Freely we have all received. And freely—without condition—we can all give away.

5

RISK OPENS THE DOOR TO THE IMPOSSIBLE

Following Jesus involves living a lifestyle of risk, but that is the kind of lifestyle He modeled for us. Risking His life and reputation from the beginning, Jesus stepped out of heaven, becoming subject to the care of His own creation as a baby born in a manger. From birth, His life was hunted as King Herod sought His death. His parents probably were scorned for having a child out of wedlock, yet this teenage peasant girl and carpenter stepfather were entrusted with raising Jesus into manhood in wisdom, knowledge and stature. He died a gruesome death on the cross, risking everything in the hope of bringing us into salvation and back to the Father.

Putting Jesus on display will always mean living a lifestyle of risk as we follow Him. The disciples were out at night fishing when they saw a man walking on the water (see Matthew 14:22–36). Terrified by what they saw, they exclaimed in fear, "It's a ghost" (verse 26). They did not realize it was Jesus in front of them. Then they heard His familiar voice saying, "Take courage! It is I. Don't be afraid" (verse 27).

Peter then said something astounding: "Lord, if it's you, tell me to come to you on the water" (verse 28). He had his doubts and knew the water was risky, but he also fully relied on Jesus and knew He could be trusted. A lifetime of fishing had taught him that if you got out of a boat away from shore, you would sink. But here was Jesus, showing him that you could walk on water.

As long as Peter kept his eyes on Jesus, he was able to walk on water. But then he started to notice his surroundings—the howling wind, the lapping water across his feet—and he began to sink as his attention was diverted from the One who could cause him to walk on water.

This is what it looks like to risk. When we don't know that Jesus is with us, we can be scared by what we see. Suddenly, even safe things feel like ghosts. And when we start focusing on what our circumstances tell us and take our eyes off the One who is with us, we will sink, just as Peter did. But when we acknowledge Jesus' presence with us, we can have confidence that the impossible is possible—not because of us, but because of the One who works the miracle.

Jesus did not call us to play it safe and stay in the boat of our comfort zone. Rather, He called us to follow Him by stepping out of the boat and into the waters of uncertainty. Risking it all for the sake of the Kingdom opens the door for the impossible to happen.

Walking on water does not happen without choosing to step into the unknown. Risk takes so many different shapes. Following Jesus often means the risk of looking foolish or embarrassing ourselves. We risk when we extend our hands to pray and hope that Jesus shows up. We risk when we put our hearts on the line to reach out to someone, knowing the person may reject us, or may reject Jesus, which feels a lot like rejecting us. We risk when we are so tangled in the worries of life that we don't feel we can spare the time or energy, and we set that feeling aside in the hope that Jesus has something better.

I believe Jesus is standing on the waters of humanity. He is beckoning the Church to step out of the boat, onto the water. The world is looking for the Church to be Jesus with skin on and to put Him on display with love and power. It will not happen without our taking a risk.

The one common thread in every encounter I have where I put Jesus on display is that it always involves risk. It is uncomfortable, uncertain and at times confusing. It causes us to be vulnerable. If Jesus does not help us walk on water, we certainly will drown. That is a scary position. It is easy to see why staying in the boat is the simpler option. But Jesus is not in the boat. Jesus is on the water.

Risk in the Midst of Hostility

Sometimes, there is a very tangible risk involved in ministering to people and spreading the good news of the Gospel. Persecution is one of the enemy's weapons against the Church. One of his tactics is to threaten physical harm, loss of possessions or security, or even death. The early Church experienced this kind of persecution in astounding ways. Stephen was the first of many martyrs (see Acts 7:54–60), and the early Christians had to learn the intricacies of following Jesus while knowing that doing so could lead to their deaths or the deaths of their loved ones.

While parts of the Church today worship at the risk of death, those of us in the Western Hemisphere experience more of a risk to our reputation, not the risk of physical harm or death. Many of us have no idea what real persecution is like. Most of us face persecution in the form of hurled words of accusation, insult and rejection, while in the rest of the world persecution takes the form not of hurled words, but of hurled stones.

Our risk of persecution often only involves a threat to how people perceive us. We risk losing credibility or relationship with someone. We risk losing people's trust if we are perceived as being fanatics or overly zealous. There is also the risk of people rejecting our message. I often wonder what would happen if real persecution came to the Western Church.

The Gospel itself carries within it a kind of foolishness. Who would believe that the Son of God would be born as a baby to a virgin, perform miracles, and then die and come back to life? To the naturally minded, it sounds like absurdity. First Corinthians 1:18 tells us, "For the message of the cross is foolishness to those who are perishing, but to us who are being saved it is the power of God." We must embrace the fact that we will be perceived as foolish if we cling to the cross. There is no way around it.

We are not promised that everything will turn out well when we take risks for Jesus. In fact, we are told that we will face hardship. In John 16:33, Jesus tells His disciples about the future difficulties they will face: "I have told you these things, so that in me you may have peace. In this world you will have trouble. But take heart! I have overcome the world." Our assurance is the peace that He brings in overcoming the world. Following Jesus will cost us something. We are also promised that Jesus will be with us in the hardship. Romans 8:35 says, "Who shall separate us from the love of Christ? Shall trouble or hardship or persecution or famine or nakedness or danger or sword?" None of those things will separate us from God's love.

A few years ago, I was ministering on the streets in a European country where I had been training my host church in how to live the "as you go" lifestyle and put Jesus on display in their city. There were many Muslim and Hindu refugees living around the particular public market area where we were, and I was eager to see the power of God break in.

"Does anyone have any pain? If you let me pray for you, I believe Jesus will heal you and show you He is real," I yelled into the crowd as I stood in the center of the market. The reaction was not what I had hoped for. Instead of eager participants, I was confronted by a mix of people—some who were completely apathetic, and some who started mocking me openly. Still, I persisted: "I believe Jesus can heal you. If you want to know that Jesus is real, I believe He will show Himself to you."

More taunts. More rejection. More people telling me to leave. I have often felt rejection when approaching people, but it is a whole different level of risk when you start to wonder if you will be confronted physically or hurt.

I noticed a young man and his girlfriend sitting in front of a restaurant. I have learned that when someone stands out in a crowd for no particular reason, it is often an indicator that the Holy Spirit is highlighting that person to me because He wants to do something. As I approached the young man, I felt I had two impressions about his life and one about a physical problem in his back. I prayed for him, and he experienced healing and God's presence. He was so touched by the experience that he asked me if I would be willing to pray for his mom, who needed a lot of help. He tried calling her, but she did not answer. I let him know that I would be in the market area for a while if she was able to show up. In case she could not, I gave him a business card for the church I was working with.

A short while later, the mom did show up. Immediately when I was introduced to her, I heard the Lord tell me to open my wallet and give her all the money I had. I did, and she broke down crying and began opening up about her life. She was the mother of several children, and the father had just abandoned them. They had no money and did not know where to go. I prayed for her and simply ministered the love of God.

Then she asked, "Could you please pray for my son?" A preteen boy stood alongside her, his face ashen and emotionless. "He just tried to kill himself last night," the mother explained. "He says he doesn't want to live anymore. We were actually just on the way to the psychiatric hospital to see if we can get him some help."

Without even thinking about it, I grabbed the boy and held him, loving on him as a dad should. I thought about my kids who were about his age. I remembered what my childhood had been like, being abandoned by my father. I poured all that compassion into this hug. I prayed over him, whispering to him about how much God loves him and has plans for his life. As I prayed, the Holy Spirit began to come on him and he started shaking. He began feeling joy as the love of God poured over him. As joy and love displaced his sorrow, I told him that he also would do what I was doing. He would proclaim the Gospel and heal the sick. He gladly gave his life to Jesus in that holy moment.

By this time, the surrounding crowd had started to notice what was happening. I told the boy that as a follower of Jesus, he could do the things that Jesus did, like heal the sick. I then asked the gathering crowd (who only minutes earlier had been mocking me) if any of them would like to experience the same power of God that had just touched this boy. As people began responding, asking for prayer, I coached him in how to pray for each person. Healings started breaking out, and people gave their lives to Jesus. So many people were coming up for prayer that we spent the next two and a half hours ministering in the market center. Several Muslims, Hindus and drunks who had previously been mocking me had now come to Christ through what had happened to this little boy who had tried to kill himself the night before. After we had prayed for everyone in the crowd, his whole family opened their hearts to Jesus.

Three years later, I was ministering again in the same country with the same group. I ran into the same boy while the church was doing outreach in the city center. We both smiled ear to ear as he ran toward me and I embraced him. His face still carried the countenance of joy rather than the weight of an abandoned child.

That afternoon, I took him out along with a group of others to pray for people and reach them with the Gospel. Taking that risk three years earlier in front of that crowd of mockers had a ripple wave of effects that continued long after I left.

Risk and Unexpected Results

I was having lunch at a Mexican restaurant with several friends, along with my three boys. I noticed the hostess and asked if I could pray for her. She had fallen recently and suffered knee pain as a result. Each time I prayed, nothing seemed to happen. She was being polite by allowing me to pray, but no healing was coming. I could tell this was going nowhere, and I was turning out to look like a fool once again. I asked if I could pray one last time. The woman agreed, clearly not expecting anything to happen.

Then another woman's voice spoke up from behind me: "I felt that!"

Not at all what I expected. "What?" I asked as I turned to see her.

A lady in a motorized wheelchair said, "I was sitting over there, and I felt a sweet presence come on me. I turned around to see what it was, and I saw that you were praying for that lady."

The woman went on to say that she had been unable to walk for more than a decade. An autoimmune disease had deteriorated the bones in her back and feet. She was in constant pain, and she was only able to move the couple of excruciating steps necessary to get into her wheelchair each day.

"Could I pray for you?" I asked. She eagerly said yes. I began to pray prayers of command: "I speak to this woman's back and legs and command them to be well. I speak strength and health into every part of her body."

I stopped and asked what she was feeling. Slowly, she was feeling her strength return. I continued praying and blessing her body, and each time she felt more and more of the power and presence of God.

After a few minutes, I asked if she was ready to try to do something she could not do before. To her shock, she was able to stand without help. We continued to pray, and she continued to gain strength. Eventually, she tried her first steps. She was timid at first, so I offered to hold her hand the whole way. Amazingly, with each step she took, she gained strength. Within moments, she was walking up and down the restaurant aisles on her own for the first time in several years!

After years of growing through my mistakes, I have learned that this strengthening process is common for people who have been disabled for many years. Very rarely have I seen someone go from completely disabled in one instant to fully able-bodied in the next. It is a gradual process. It is a "working of miracles." Often, these kinds of physical disabilities come with their fair share of debilitating mindsets. These people have difficulty believing that God could do such a dramatic healing. So I offer to support their weight as they take their first steps, gradually working toward just holding their hands, and eventually making it all the way to cheering them on as they walk on their own with confidence. The miracle has to be worked out while Jesus also heals their hearts and minds.

"My back was hurting so badly," this woman said through her tears, "and now I don't have any pain!" She was stunned by being healed and being able to walk without assistance. We kept walking up and down in the restaurant as I continued to pray and bless her body.

"Oh wow, it feels so good," she said. "I'm not stooping or hunched over! I can walk without holding on to anything or stumbling! I've got chills going all through me." Slowly, the reality and implications of the miracle she had experienced began to sink in. "I can stand up and do my own dishes now. I can go to my friend's house and just walk into the room." Her whole world had changed.

I had risked it by stepping out to pray for the hostess. It appeared that nothing happened with her, but God used my simple risk with one woman to open the door to the impossible for another. A little while later, as we were getting ready to leave, I saw the woman who had been healed standing up in the restaurant and telling everyone who would listen about how God had healed her.

Dealing with Failure

Without taking a risk when we put Jesus on display with love and power, we will never see the sick healed or the brokenhearted comforted or people come to faith in Christ. But risk is never absent of fear, failure or being denied. We will miss it. We will fail. There will be times when the Good News just flat-out will not be received. This is just truth. It may be due to a combination of factors. It may be that we need more growth on our end. Some of it is opposition from the enemy, or the hardening of another person's heart. Sometimes, we are just planting and watering a seed, so to speak. No matter the reason our attempts may occasionally fall flat, know this: The Kingdom is at hand, and our job is to love, be bold, take risks, grow and try to hear God and love people. Whenever we miss it or fail, or when the gift of His Good News is not received, we simply keep living it and pressing into Jesus and His commissioning.

No one bats a thousand, but that does not mean we don't try to swing the bat. If we fail, it does not mean we are out of the game. It simply means we just pick up the bat and swing again. I might not ever bat a thousand, but either way my, goal is to remember I have been commissioned to play Kingdom ball, swing that bat and get my eyes off me and onto Jesus and His mission.

One day, two friends and I decided to go out on the streets in the small town my friend lived in to do power evangelism. We started the day in prayer and full of faith. I even received incredibly specific words of knowledge for a particular woman we saw across the street. Unfortunately, she left before we could speak with her, but we hoped we would see her again later. We headed out the door fully expecting to see many people radically touched by God and saved.

We started out at a coffee shop, where we attempted to share some words of knowledge with the barista. We failed so severely that she told me I was pretty bad at this. Discouraged but not deterred, we headed to an apartment complex, where we started going door to door, asking if we could pray for people. We heard a lot of "No, thank you" and "Nobody's home." One guy told us we needed to go back home and pray some more. It was a real faith killer. When the lost tell you that your prophetic ministry is bad, it feels as if it is time to go home.

Sometimes the enemy's war tactic is to assault you with the voice of condemnation, labeling you as a failure and taking away your confidence in the mercy, mission and good news of the Kingdom. He is masterful at this. These fiery thoughts and feelings are masked to get you to own them as your own, and it can be very hard at times to discern in the moment and not be captivated by his weapons of war.

In Joshua 1:9, God tells Joshua, "Be strong and courageous. Do not be afraid; do not be discouraged, for the LORD your God will be with you wherever you go." We have a choice. We can stay in fear and discouragement, or we can choose to be strong and courageous. Even when we don't feel strong, we can choose it, knowing that God is with us wherever we go.

But we also often have to struggle against internal risk—the risk of confronting our own doubts and questions. This is actually a common form of risk that I experience. I question whether or not I am hearing from God. I question whether God wants to heal people. I question my ability to know what to say or do. I question my motives.

Not only do I question a lot of things, I also feel a lot of things. I feel anxious. I feel discouraged before I even try. I feel the threat of rejection, and I start bracing myself for how to respond to it. I feel insufficient. I feel too tired or distracted or busy. I feel unqualified and disqualified.

Experience also has shown me that there is always tension, struggle and war from the enemy, who is trying to feed me full of doubt so I don't take that step of faith in love. This opposition can deter you when doubts swirl inside your mind—or you can view it as an indication that you are on to something. Opposition is often a sign that the Kingdom of God is about to break in. But even knowing this does not make it easy or prevent the internal struggle with doubt.

Finally, at the end of that long, difficult day out praying with my friends with no results, we came back to my friend's house to lick our wounds. We were giving ourselves the "at least we tried" pep talk when something shifted. We were filled with faith that God was still doing something. I looked out the window and saw a group of people standing around, the same people who were with the woman I had gotten words for earlier. We walked out to the group and described the woman, asking if they knew her. I told them I believed I had a message from God for her. That got their attention, and they called her for me. I introduced myself over the phone and began sharing the specific prophetic words. The words were all accurate, and the woman wept as she was touched by the power of God. She started making arrangements to meet us at the house with her boyfriend.

During this time, my friends started ministering to the other people who were gathered at the house. The atmosphere had completely shifted, and the power of God was tangible and thick. God's presence was radically touching these men. Long story short, by the end, a man who was going blind had his sight completely restored. · We were able to minister to the woman, and her boyfriend was healed from a painful shoulder injury that had kept him from being able to work. We prayed with another man, and God miraculously showed him a supernatural sign of His love. The power of God was moving so strongly that one man said, "It felt like I was being tasered!" He then gave his heart to Jesus.

The woman and her boyfriend had to be somewhere right away, so we quickly prayed that Jesus would come near to them, and we told them He loved them. They received everything we were saying and thanked us as they left. Everyone was amazed by what had happened.

The day had started out with lots of hope, followed by the crushing feeling of failure, but it ended with people's lives being changed. We risked a lot that day, and we initially felt as though we had failed. We had doors slammed in our faces at the apartment complexes, and we failed at every attempt we made to minister to people. But in the end, the Kingdom of God came and Jesus was put on display with love and power.

Risk Involves Tension

Just because you step out in risk does not mean the results will be what you expected or hoped for. There will be times you see healings happen instantly, progressively or not at all. You will see more as you step out, and will see nothing if you don't risk anything. The reality is that I am more shocked now when I don't see someone healed than when I do, and I am always like a kid on Christmas when I do see the in-break of God's Kingdom come upon people and they are set free, healed or loved on by His presence. But nonetheless, risk would not be risk if there were not a real chance of failure.

Years ago, I got a phone call that a family friend was dying from cirrhosis of the liver. This was a woman I had known since my childhood, and I knew she did not have a relationship with Jesus. She had been bound by alcohol her whole life. I asked my mentor, Charles Bello, to come with me to the hospital to pray for her. Ten feet from her hospital room, I could smell the alcohol emanating from her dying body as she lay in a coma. Her family was gathered in her room, praying for a miracle.

Charles and I began to pray, asking Jesus to heal her. As we prayed, she immediately awoke and opened her eyes. Her whole family was shocked at this. Was God healing her?

I looked into her eyes and said, "Jesus loves you. He's pursuing your heart. He wants a relationship with you. Would you like to give your heart to Jesus?"

She was too weak to talk, but she looked at me with tears in her eyes as she nodded in agreement.

I said, "I'm going to pray for Jesus to come into your heart. If you agree, just squeeze my hand and nod."

She squeezed my hand and nodded as I prayed a prayer of salvation over her. As tears streamed down her face, a peace and tranquility fell over her entire body. Her eyes closed, and she slipped right back into the coma. She never awoke from the coma and died the next day.

I had so wanted to see our family friend healed. I had wanted her to rise up from the bed with a new liver. I was so thankful that she had come to know Jesus and was now in heaven with Him, but I had wanted her to be alive and well here on earth as a testimony of God's healing power. Yet that did not happen.

Why share this with you? Because if you choose to step out and risk it, this will be part of the journey. Some people I know get uncomfortable talking about these kinds of things or encourage me not to share them because it does not build faith. I think it hinders faith, however, not to share the struggle. Over the years, I have prayed for more people than I can count. I have seen a lot of amazing healings and salvations. But I have also seen a lot of people not get healed, deteriorate and die, and even get healed and then still die.

A good friend has often told me, "Even though Jesus raised Lazarus from the dead, he still died again." But Lazarus will also rise again because Jesus is the Resurrection. Complete healing does not come until we are with Jesus in heaven. We live in tension and this can be hard to wrap our minds around, so we come up with pat theological answers that do more harm than good on either end of the spectrum. If we are honest, we are all growing in our understanding of His Kingdom and practice.

This tension arises from the tangled factors we contend with, as I mentioned, which can include spiritual war and opposition from the enemy, the hardness of people's hearts, and our own faith struggle and lack of understanding. There is also the mystery of the now and not yet of the Kingdom. Looking into each of these factors can provide some perspective on our experiences (or lack of experience) with healing, but they can also become excuses that we allow to prevent us from stepping out in risk. Stepping out and doing Kingdom ministry is one of the most fulfilling and rewarding activities, however, because that is what we were made for—to put His image on display to others, to be fruitful, multiply and subdue the earth. We are to expand the garden of His delight everywhere we go.

I believe it is Jesus' will to heal, just as I believe it is Jesus' will that all people would come to a saving faith in His love. Yet sometimes God's will does not happen. I know a statement like that can scare people, but if we look in the Bible, we find many examples of people not receiving God's love and Kingdom, and we find Jesus' disciples not being able to heal everyone who came to them. He rebuked His disciples when they could not heal the sick. Ouch! Everyone who came to Jesus was healed. Even in the case when His disciples could not heal the sick boy, Jesus stepped in and healed him. Jesus' will is to heal. We cannot allow our unanswered questions and unanswered prayers to form a theology that leads us into playing it safe and not living a lifestyle of love that takes risks.

Risk also involves being in the uncomfortable tension of not having all the answers. Rather than offering trite religious platitudes, I have gotten more comfortable with saying "I don't know," and then asking for more revelation and power to walk like Jesus.

We also need to learn to mourn with those who mourn, to help the dying die well with love and comfort, and to listen to God's heart and have the boldness even to raise the dead—not from our desperate wishes or wants, but from His commissioning. This stuff is messy to our unrenewed minds, and we have to wrestle with these questions.

We will live in tension on this side of heaven, but may we also grow in compassion, wisdom, love, boldness and risk. May we mourn rightly, and may we rejoice that His Kingdom has come, is coming and will one day fully come. Our job is simply to look, listen and respond to His calling, which is always love coupled with His power to heal or comfort. There is more of the now of the Kingdom than we think. The tension of the not yet is never a free pass or an excuse not to live the Gospel. We will simply have to be comfortable living in the radical middle as heaven is invading earth through us, even as we mature as sons and daughters of God who still have clay feet and unrenewed minds.

When we face difficult situations, we have to choose how we respond to our own disappointed hopes. We face a couple of options when nothing seems to happen in response to our prayers. One, we could get super discouraged, which is almost always my biggest temptation. I think to myself, *I'm not going to risk it again. This is foolish, and maybe it's not God's will to heal.*

Or two, the other option is to think, *Okay, I'm not sure why nothing seemed to happen. Holy Spirit, is there anything I need to learn from this? Lord, give me more boldness and love to keep stepping out. Open my eyes and heart for more.* Then we make the choice either to quit or to look for other opportunities to demonstrate His love and power.

It is normal to feel discouragement and to ask questions, as long as your questions don't lead you into doubting the goodness of God and His commissioning. Turn those questions to Jesus, not away from Him. I love what I heard someone say once: "Focus on what God is doing, not on what we don't see Him doing." It is only by looking at Jesus that we can have the boldness to risk again.

Growing in a lifestyle of power evangelism is a learning process that will involve many perceived failures, which can become discouraging if we don't realize that success in the Kingdom is measured by our obedience. The more we step out in obedience to God's invitation, the more we will grow through those experiences. I have been doing power evangelism for twenty years now, and I am still constantly learning and growing. I am attempting new approaches and models, and I am trying new things. I am seeing what works and what does not. In other words, I am practicing being a learner.

It is said that practice makes perfect. It is true that the only way to become better at something is to practice. I think it might be better, however, to state it a little differently: Don't practice being perfect and being an expert, but rather, practice being proficient. We have too many experts who have actually stopped being practitioners. Practitioners practice!

Taking a posture of learning takes the pressure off trying to get it right every time. Each time we miss a word of knowledge or stumble over our words as we approach someone, we can learn from the situation and adapt so that we do it better next time. Practice never makes you perfect; it just makes you more proficient.

Try setting the goal of practicing. I have a friend who is trying to grow in risk-taking and in putting Jesus on display. She told me, "I'm setting a risk quota for my life." Her risk quota is to take one risk in healing the sick or seeing people come to faith each week. That is four to five acts of risk a month. What she thought might seem simple or like baby steps was to me brilliance! What may seem like a crawl to her is actually training her to run a marathon. It does not matter where you start—just start.

I hope I always keep my heart in a learning posture and practice what I preach. I hope I always keep growing as a learner in the subjects where I think I have gained any insight. I want to enjoy growing in more simplicity as a practitioner who gets his hands dirty in the soil of sowing and cultivating, rather than planting plastic plants that look perfect but have no life or ability to reproduce. There is a beauty in being simply ordinary—more concerned with practicing to learn than with being a perfect expert who can only really impart a glare of self-righteousness. Many experts look down on you with their accomplishments instead of reaching out a hand to show you how to shovel through the dirt of the trials, joys, mistakes and hardships along the way. Rather, I choose to enjoy the beauty of practicing being a learner, not practicing being perfect.

Risk Confronts Fear and Builds Faith

Faith is like a muscle; it has to be built up by repeated use. Fear is the enemy's tactic to keep us from engaging our faith and stepping out in risk. It would not feel fearful if there was not a real chance that something could go wrong. People may not want to engage in conversation. They may refuse prayer. I may stumble over my words, not knowing what to say. When I do say something, it may be the wrong thing and I may make Jesus look bad. If nothing happens when I pray, the person may move further away from Christ, not toward Him. Fear is the underlying common theme in all these concerns. And they are usually the enemy's mirage to keep our eyes from the possibilities of what could happen if we do step out in risk.

Our greatest weapon against fear is love. "There is no fear in love. But perfect love drives out fear" (1 John 4:18). Our love for others and love for Christ can give us what we need to overcome fear. Our enemy ministers fear to keep both us and the person we are ministering to bound. Instead of giving in to that fear, we face it with love.

Risk always causes my knees to knock, heart to pound, body to sweat and stomach to turn. Risk demands dealing with thoughts and feelings of awkwardness and embarrassment if I blow it. There is no way around all of this. The only way is to face it head on with love, and to trust the Holy Spirit to take even my mess and work it into an encounter, despite whether or not I miss it. And even if I miss it, at least I was exercising my faith and not giving in to fear.

The enemy will do whatever he can to make your fear bigger than Jesus. Putting Jesus on display does not mean you don't experience fear or feel the sting of it. You just don't let it form you into its image. Let it be a faith builder. Press through those distractions and look for an opportunity to put Jesus on display with love and power.

Fear is such an illusion anyway, isn't it? Someone once said, "Fear is faith pointing in the wrong direction." Or as another person said, "Fear is *False Evidence Appearing Real*." But the enemy always blows those moments up, as if they are the end of the world. I might look like a fool, but at least I am being a fool for Christ, and God loves to take the foolish things of the world to confound the wise (see 1 Corinthians 1:27). It is a sign of the in-breaking of the Kingdom.

Success in the Kingdom is obedience—taking that step of risk, dying to yourself, and at times looking foolish. Isn't that what Jesus did? He died on the cross, beaten and naked, marred beyond recognition. That looked like foolishness and defeat to the world and the enemy, but Jesus' death became our resurrection and life. What appeared to be His foolishness became our healing and forgiveness, and it brought us into righteousness and relationship with the Father. Looking foolish is part of the deal when stepping out in risk. If the Father allowed Jesus to look foolish by dying on a cross, then what makes us think we won't look like fools? John

Wimber used to say, "I'm a fool for Christ. Whose fool are you?" What looks like foolishness to the world just might be the way of salvation and healing for the world.

Putting Jesus on display means risking looking foolish so that others might encounter Jesus and His Kingdom. We can pick up the bat and swing for home runs—salvations, healings and seeing the demonized freed—but don't be discouraged and quit when you don't see the results you hope for. Don't make excuses, either. Be honest and transparent, and get back into the game. Step up to the plate and play Kingdom ball for Him, so that others might be freed to run home into the loving arms of the Father.

Remember, you will strike out, you will fail, you will walk, you will get hit, and you will get spitballs and curve balls thrown at you. But you will also get on base, and you just might hit a lot of home runs. Either way, the Kingdom of God is at hand. And we can always pick up the bat again.

Two decades of practice have given me lots of opportunities for missteps, mistakes and failures. But they have also shown me that taking those risks often opens the door to the impossible and to an opportunity to put Jesus on display. I have learned that if I say nothing, nothing will happen. That is a 100 percent certainty that there is no risk there. And if I do say something and nothing happens, at least I was putting my faith into practice.

As John Wimber often said, faith will always be spelled R-I-S-K! Step out of your comfy boat and onto the water. You might sink and get wet, but you just might find yourself walking on water with Jesus. Success in the Kingdom is measured by our obedience. Failure in the Kingdom is simply staying in the boat, huddled in your own fear. So what if you and I get wet trying to walk on water? I have gotten wet a bunch of times, and I have learned to swim in those awkward moments. But I can tell you this: There is nothing better than stepping out of the boat and walking on water with Jesus. Risk opens the door to the impossible!

6

LOOK, LISTEN AND RESPOND

Several years ago, I was praying as I was just going about a normal day and I heard the Holy Spirit speak to me. He said, *Brian, all I want is for you to do three things: look, listen and respond.*

That is all. Nothing more, or more complicated. He was telling me simply to respond to what I see Him doing or hear Him saying. That simple phrase—look, listen and respond—helped demystify power evangelism for me. Those three steps are things anybody can do. Any of us can learn to look for the Holy Spirit's activity around us, listen to His voice and respond in simple obedience. It can happen anytime and anywhere, whether we are on a phone call, going through a drive-thru or shopping at the mall.

How do we develop a lifestyle of looking, listening and responding? Since the Holy Spirit gave me those three words as a guidepost, I have been on this journey of learning to partner with Him by simply looking, listening and responding to His activity. He is always at work around us. We know that He is actively involved in the lives of every person we pass on the street, every client we interact with at work and every shopper we see when we buy groceries or gas. We don't bring ministry to any situation; God is already doing that. We don't carry the burden of "bringing Jesus" with us; He is already there. All we have to do is to look and listen to where He is already active, and then respond by joining Him in His activity.

Shifting Mindsets

If we shift our mindset to joining Jesus where He is already active instead of trying to make something happen on our own, then we realize that all we have to do is be available to God. My good friend Robby Dawkins puts it this way: Jesus puts His ability on our availability. Again, we don't bring ministry; we step into the ministry that is already happening by making ourselves available to God.

When Jesus and the disciples were faced with a hungry crowd gathering around them, one of the disciples asked, "Here is a boy with five small barley loaves and two small fish, but how far will they go among so many?" (John 6:9). The story continues:

> Jesus said, "Have the people sit down." There was plenty of grass in that place, and they sat down (about five thousand men were there). Jesus then took the loaves, gave thanks, and distributed to those who were seated as much as they wanted. He did the same with the fish.
>
> When they had all had enough to eat, he said to his disciples, "Gather the pieces that are left over. Let nothing be wasted." So they gathered them and filled twelve baskets with the pieces of the five barley loaves left over by those who had eaten.
>
> John 6:10–13

The boy's loaves and fish were not enough to feed the crowd. But when he brought what he had, Jesus added the miracle. Likewise, when the disciples were passing out the food, there was not enough of it to accommodate the need. But as they handed it out, the loaves and fish were multiplied to the point that a surplus was left over. That boy and the disciples made available to Jesus what they had, and the miracle was displayed as that small lunch passed through their hands. The key was being available to respond to what God wanted to do supernaturally through them.

This mindset of availability and response is how Jesus did ministry. He tells us in John 5:19–20,

> Very truly I tell you, the Son can do nothing by himself; he can do only what he sees his Father doing, because whatever the Father does the Son also does. For the Father loves the Son and shows him all he does. Yes, and he will show him even greater works than these, so that you will be amazed.

Even Jesus did not act on His own; He started by doing only what He saw the Father doing. He simply joined the Father in His work. Likewise, we need to train ourselves to look and see what the Father is doing.

We must remember that ministry is service to another person. The heart of the Father is to serve and redeem humanity back to Himself. Mark 10:45 tells us, "For even the Son of Man did not come to be served, but to serve, and to give his life as a ransom for many." As Jesus lays down His life on behalf of the people around us, He invites us to join Him in that mission.

One helpful analogy is a United Parcel Service (UPS) delivery person. When you get a package, it is not from the UPS person; it is from the sender. The UPS person simply delivers what someone else wants you to have. When we approach our day as UPS delivery people waiting for packages from God to deliver to people He loves, we have shifted our mindset to serving those around us. We are not the One who heals or sets free or saves; we are simply God's UPS delivery service, responding to what He wants to do. As we make ourselves available, the Father delivers

His packages through us. All we have to do is look and listen for the packages and respond in obedience, delivering what He wants to give.

When we listen, we are listening in two directions: to God and to the person we are ministering to. We can receive insightful information both ways. God can give us supernatural revelation into what He wants to do or how He wants us to pray. The person gives us key information about the situation, concern or health problem he or she wants prayer for. Both kinds of listening are critical, and learning to listen well in both directions can help us become more competent in praying effective prayers by partnering with what God is doing in the person's life.

Look and Listen with Compassion

The biggest obstacle we have today in learning to look and listen is our own busyness. When we are not entrenched in an activity, we distract ourselves with phone calls or podcasts or social media. The first step in being able to join Jesus in His activity around us is to give our attention to it. Be intentional as you go about your day. Look and listen to what is happening around you. What do you see and hear? Who stands out to you? Whom do you feel drawn to? What needs do you see? We will never be able to do what the Father is doing if we don't first take time to see or hear it.

The biggest way I have found to be able to look and listen for the Holy Spirit's activity is to notice where I feel compassion. Jesus did this in Matthew 9:36: "When he saw the crowds, he had compassion on them, because they were harassed and helpless, like sheep without a shepherd." In the same way, when we feel moved with compassion, it is often a sign of God's activity on people and His desire to minister to them. Look for where you feel faith or sense that someone is highlighted and stands out to you. You can also look for where you simply see a person in need.

Follow the heart of compassion. It is often an indicator that the Holy Spirit wants to do something, and He is just waiting for us to respond and join Him.

One day I had taken my mother to a doctor's appointment and was waiting in the parking garage outside, passing the time by talking on the phone to my friend. I happened to look up and see a lady walking with difficulty toward the parking garage. I felt compassion for her. "Sorry," I interrupted my friend, "I have to let you go. I'll call you right back."

I knew the compassion I felt was an invitation to respond to Jesus' activity in this woman's life. I did not yet know what God was going to do, but I knew I wanted to respond by joining Him. I approached her and asked, "Are you okay?"

"No, I'm in a lot of pain. I had a horrible infection in my leg, and the doc tried to remove the infection." She went on to explain that she was very worried and still in tremendous pain. When I asked her on a scale from zero to ten what her pain level was, she said, "It's a ten!"

I said, "This may sound crazy to you—I don't know—but I'm a follower of Jesus. Could I pray for you?" She gladly agreed. I asked if I could put my hand on her shoulder, and then I began to tell the pain and infection to go. I could see tears rolling down her face, so I asked her what she was experiencing.

"I feel a warm presence coming all over my body," she replied.

I smiled and said, "That's the Lord." I blessed the work of God's Spirit on her and once again told the pain and infection to go.

Through her tears she said, "All the pain is totally gone!" She started moving around, doing things that would have really hurt before.

Then the Lord gave me an impression that something was going on in her family that really troubled her. I shared that with her.

"That's right," she said. "It's about one of my kids." She began to weep, this time from emotional pain.

I prayed for her and spoke peace over the family situation. I asked Jesus for wisdom and healing in that relationship. She continued experiencing God's activity and healing as He ministered to her deep wound and burden.

My heart was moved with compassion because I saw this woman's physical pain. That compassion was an invitation to partner with God. Not only did God want to heal her body, He also wanted to bring healing to her heart and relationships. All I did was look at her and see her pain, listen to the compassion stirring inside and respond in simple obedience by asking if she was okay. The results were up to God. I simply joined in what He already wanted to do.

It is not all that hard to look and listen. Where we often get hung up is the response part. We are too busy, or we don't know what to do. Responding is not easy. Responding means taking a risk. It means taking unplanned time out of our day. It means interrupting a phone call with a friend to talk to a lady in pain. It is faith in action. Responding does not mean we have faith in our own abilities. All it means is that we simply make ourselves available for God's ability to break in on behalf of someone else.

Look and Listen in Supernatural Ways

One of the ways we can learn to look and listen is supernaturally. There are many ways in which God speaks. Job 33:14 says, "For God does speak—now one way, now another—though no one perceives it." The passage goes on to list some of the ways God speaks: He can speak through dreams, in visions, in our ears or through our circumstances.

John 10:27–28 compares us to sheep and Jesus to a shepherd. It tells us that the sheep know the voice of their shepherd, and they won't follow the voice of another. Every follower of Jesus is capable of hearing and understanding Jesus' voice and the various ways it comes.

Not only does God speak to us personally, but He also speaks to us on behalf of others as He invites us into His mission. God could give us a word of knowledge, a prophetic word or an impression about a person or a situation. A word of knowledge is supernatural revelation about a person, condition or situation that you could not have known otherwise. As we learn to hear God's voice in these ways, it imparts faith to us that God wants to do something for a person. It can also be a very helpful way to approach someone. (You will find a more detailed explanation of how you may receive words of knowledge and how to approach people with them in chapter 10, "A Healing and Power Evangelism Model.")

Supernatural revelation often comes as fleeting thoughts, not as a booming voice. In 1 Kings 19:11–12, Elijah experienced God's voice in this quiet way:

> Then a great and powerful wind tore the mountains apart and shattered the rocks before the LORD, but the LORD was not in the wind. After the wind there was an earthquake, but the LORD was not in the earthquake. After the earthquake came a fire, but the LORD was not in the fire. And after the fire came a gentle whisper.

On rare occasions, we may hear God in a booming way, but most often, His voice will come quietly and fleetingly. We must have an awareness and sensitivity to the Holy Spirit to hear His voice and not miss it. The good news is that we can train ourselves to learn to be sensitive to these impressions, and we can gain confidence in acting on them. The more we respond when we think God is speaking to us, the better we get at recognizing His voice when it comes.

Here is an example of looking and listening in a supernatural way. I was running errands with my mom, and we stopped at a pharmacy to pick up a prescription. I had been telling her all about putting Jesus on display, sharing words of knowledge and people getting healed. As we parked, I happened to look over to my left and saw a woman sitting in her car. Her window was down, and I had an impression that something was wrong with one entire side of her body. It was a fleeting thought, but I stepped out and took a risk.

In other words, I did not just look and listen; I had to respond to see if what I thought I had received was correct. I said, "Excuse me, ma'am. You're experiencing pain all throughout one side of your body."

My mom squirmed in her seat as she whispered, "This is awkward. . . ." But I could tell that because of the stories I had been telling her, she was also curious to see what God might do.

Completely shocked, the lady in the other car looked at me and said, "Yes, that's right. How did you know?"

"Ma'am, this may seem crazy, but sometimes Jesus speaks to me about conditions in people's bodies. I'm a follower of Jesus. Could I pray for you?"

"Sure you can," she said cautiously. As I got out of the car and went over, she told me she had just come from the doctor. The whole side of her body was painful, from her arm down into her hip and leg. On a scale from zero to ten, she said the pain was a level eight.

"I'm going to pray for you right here," I told her.

"Whoa, hold on a second. You aren't going to lay hands on me, are you?" she asked. "Because I heard that in the Bible it says if someone lays hands on you, you could get an evil spirit."

I just smiled and said, "It's okay. I want you to feel comfortable." I backed several feet away and stuck my hands in my pockets to seem as unthreatening as possible. "I'm just going to stay over here and ask the Holy Spirit to come heal your body. You're going to feel a warmth flow through you as a sign of God's presence on you."

I began to pray by simply speaking to the pain and telling it to go. Then I asked, "What are you experiencing?"

She said, "I feel a warm tingling sensation all over that side." She started to move her arm up and was shocked. "I couldn't lift it this high before!"

"But you're still feeling the pain down your hip into your leg, right?" I asked. She said yes, so I spoke to her hip and leg again, commanded the pain to go and blessed the presence of the Lord on her. Again, she said she felt more warmth and tingling, and then the pain all went away.

"Let's really check to see if it's all gone," I suggested. "Try to do something you couldn't do before."

She stepped out of the car. "I can hardly walk, and I'm always in pain when I do." But she timidly took some first steps, and within seconds she started walking pain free, with a normal gait.

I asked how long it had been since she could walk with no pain.

"A long time," she replied. "I hardly walk anywhere. Maybe to the porch, and that's it." She explained that she had sent her sister into the pharmacy to get her medications because she could not walk well and was in so much pain. But now the pain was gone, and she was smiling and saying, "Now I can walk into the store myself!"

As we all walked in the door together, we saw her sister, who immediately said, "What are you doing? You can't walk!"

"You're right, I couldn't till this guy prayed for me and Jesus healed me," she said.

Her sister was taken aback, trying to wrap her mind around what she was seeing and hearing. "I'm glad Jesus healed you," she said, "because the pharmacist just denied your prescription. We would have driven all the way home with you still in pain."

As I looked at the sister, I could tell she was curious. I wondered if she wanted to ask for prayer herself, so I asked her.

"Yes! I'm in so much pain, too," she answered. "I have more than one chronic illness, and I hurt all the time." She said her pain was a seven or eight on a scale from zero to ten.

"Let's pray for you, then." I called my mom over and said, "Mom, come help me heal this woman."

My mom had never done anything like this before, but I was proud of her. She came right over without any hesitation, and we asked the lady if we could put our hands on her. She agreed, so my mom put her hand on the lady's shoulder. I said, "Mom, pray like this: Tell the pain to go."

My mom very compassionately and sweetly told the pain to go and asked Jesus to let healing come. I also spoke to the pain and commanded it to leave, and then I asked the lady what she felt.

"I don't really know how to describe it," she said. "It's a numb, tingling feeling coming all over me."

We prayed blessing over what the Holy Spirit was doing, and all the pain soon left. She started bending down and kicking her legs. She was so overwhelmed by the love of God that she broke down and started crying.

I told her how much Jesus loved her, and she asked, "Can I give you a hug?" My mom and I hugged her and thanked Jesus for healing her. Two women were healed and set free from physical pain and bondage simply because I took the time to look, listen and respond.

Look and Listen in Natural Ways

I often have people tell me that the reason they don't pray for people or their healing is because they don't get words of knowledge. They feel as though they have to have a supernatural word from God before they can pray for someone. Their hesitation is understandable, but it overlooks the fact that we can also look and listen with our natural senses to see God's activity around us. When Jesus healed blind Bartimaeus, He did not get a word of knowledge about this man's blindness. Jesus simply heard him crying out and saw that he was blind, so He healed him (see Mark 10:46–52). We can do the same thing. Looking and listening for God's activity around us does not have to be a mystical experience. It can be completely natural.

Jeremiah also experienced God speaking to him through completely natural means, and he used those natural prompts to give highly accurate and profound prophetic words. Jeremiah 1:11–13 records such an event:

> The word of the LORD came to me: "What do you see, Jeremiah?"
> "I see the branch of an almond tree," I replied.
> The LORD said to me, "You have seen correctly, for I am watching to see that my word is fulfilled."
> The word of the LORD came to me again: "What do you see?"
> "I see a pot that is boiling," I answered. "It is tilting toward us from the north."

In this situation God used the prophet's natural observations—an almond tree branch and a boiling pot—to speak to him about what He was going to do with the kingdoms in the north. All because Jeremiah simply looked at what was around him and allowed God to use his natural senses to speak to him.

When I first started learning about God's desire to heal today and the theology of His Kingdom, I started getting lots of words of knowledge supernaturally. I eventually got very comfortable recognizing a word of knowledge, especially for healing. I became confident that God would heal someone when I first felt I had a word of knowledge about the condition. Over the years since then, I have come to learn that healings and salvations also occur just as often when I look and listen naturally. We don't have to be limited by hearing a word from the Lord before we step out in compassion and respond by partnering with Jesus in His activity.

For example, when my family and I took a day trip to an indoor water park, I happened to see a lady wearing a neck brace. She was floating near us in the lazy river. I asked her why she had the brace and if she was in pain. She said she had recently undergone major surgery involving fusions in her neck.

I asked her what her level of pain was on a scale from zero to ten. She said it had been an eight or higher since the surgery. I asked if I could pray for her. She said yes and that she was also a believer.

I prayed as we floated down the lazy river, and the pain decreased from an eight to a four. I prayed again, and this time it dropped to a two. The third time I prayed, the pain completely left.

"There's no more pain! It's totally gone," she exclaimed. She had not been pain free in over a month.

"What were you feeling when I prayed for you?" I asked.

"It was a warm feeling, as if a hand were touching my neck. Then the pain left."

All of this happened while we were floating around the lazy river. My kids were with me, and as soon as the prayer was over, we continued enjoying our day out as a family. I had not been asking God for words of knowledge for people He wanted to heal. I was not even purposefully trying to minister to anyone. My mission was simply to enjoy a day with my kids. But I also used my natural eyes and saw a natural need. I used that cue of seeing someone in need as an invitation from the Lord to respond.

Another example of looking and listening in the natural happened one day as I was checking into a hotel with two of my kids. I noticed a hotel employee who was limping. He looked as if one of his legs was giving him pain.

"Excuse me, sir. I noticed you are limping," I said. "Are you all right?"

"Yes," he explained, "it's just the arthritis in my knee. It's acting up today with the weather change."

His name tag said Charles. I began to ask him a few questions about how long he had had the pain and what his pain level was. "Would you like me to help take that pain away?" I asked.

Charles looked at me strangely, and I explained further: "I'm a Christian, and I believe God will heal you if I pray."

"Sure, young man. You can pray for me," he said as he began to turn and walk away. Clearly, he was expecting me to pray quietly on my own time.

I was determined not to let the opportunity pass, so right before he walked away, I began to pray out loud, "Jesus, would You come and heal this man's knee now? I speak to the arthritis and pain and command them to leave now, in Jesus' name."

I could see the surprise in his eyes that I was actually serious about praying for him right there in public. "Thank you," he said a little dismissively. I watched him leave, and after about three steps his entire body started to gyrate. He stopped and looked back at me with a *what's going on?* expression. He kept walking away, and again after about the third step, his whole body and leg shook. Every few steps another jolt would hit him. He walked across the lobby, turned around and walked back.

"Young man, I think your prayer worked."

I began to explain that it was Jesus. "God is pursuing you. He loves you. He healed you to show you He's here and wants a relationship with you."

Here I was in this supernatural moment, when I was suddenly thrust back into a very natural moment as my son blurted, "Daddy, I gotta go to the bathroom! I gotta go now!"

I looked over at Charles, who said with a grin, "Well, when you gotta go, you gotta go."

I excused myself and rushed my son to the nearest restroom. I decided to use the facilities, too, while we were there. Standing at the urinal, I decided to do what any evangelist would do—strike up a conversation with the guy next to me.

The guy responded by saying, "Man, I hope this weather clears up. It's my birthday this weekend, and the cold is aggravating my neck and shoulder."

Huh, I thought to myself, *what if this is another opportunity just like with Charles out in the lobby?* I could see this man also had on a staff uniform, as if he worked in the hotel kitchen. I asked him what was wrong with his neck and shoulder, and he said an old football injury from decades ago still flared up with the cold weather.

"Hey, do you know Charles, the concierge who walks with a limp?" I asked him.

"Yeah, I know Charles."

"Well, he doesn't walk with a limp anymore."

"What?!" I could see the guy's eyes widen.

"Yeah, I just prayed for him, and all the pain left his knee. He doesn't limp anymore."

"No kidding!"

"Would you like me to pray for your shoulder and neck? I believe that just as Jesus healed Charles's knee, He can heal you. But I think we should wash our hands first," I said with a smirk. (After all, cleanliness is next to godliness!)

My son also joined us—after washing his hands—and we prayed a short prayer commanding the pain to go in Jesus' name. Immediately, all the pain left. I asked the man to move his shoulder and neck around and test them out. He told me the pain was completely gone and he had not felt that good in years.

Again, both these men were healed as a result of my just looking and listening in a natural way. I saw Charles's limp, and I heard the other man complain about his neck and shoulder pain. I did not see a supernatural glory cloud hovering over Charles when I walked into the hotel, and I did not hear an angel talking to me at the urinal. I simply used my natural eyes and ears, and God used that as a supernatural invitation to join Him in what He was doing in these men's lives.

Look, Listen and Respond over the Phone

I have learned that phone sales calls or customer service calls don't have to be an annoying hassle. They can be an opportunity to look, listen and respond. I had called a cellular company to switch services to their international plan for an upcoming mission trip. After about ten minutes with the agent on the phone, I knew the call was coming to an end. Just before wrapping up, I silently asked Jesus if there was anything He wanted to show me about the agent, and I sensed a faint impression that I thought might be from Him. I said to her, "Before you go, do you mind if I ask you a question? I often get pictures or impressions about things that are going on in people's lives, mostly connected to physical conditions. It's a gift."

That may sound as if I were full of confidence, but the reality is that I have learned how to put on a good game face over the years. Every time I initiate a conversation about healing, a word of knowledge or the Gospel, I feel a thousand butterflies hit my stomach. I have learned not to succumb to the feeling, and I actually have come to appreciate it. It means that every time I "step out of the boat" and take a risk, as Peter did, I need to keep my eyes on Jesus.

I continued, "The picture and impression I have for you is a physical one. I saw you had pain throughout your entire body—your joints, your muscles, your neck and back—all through your whole body."

The woman immediately responded to the word of knowledge. "Oh my gosh, it's all true! How do you know?"

"I'll tell you in just a second. Do you have a condition like fibromyalgia or something?" I was guessing at this, but I knew the impression I was getting had to do with pain in her joints and muscles.

She said, "No, I was just recently diagnosed with a different condition that affects my whole body, just as you were saying. In fact, right when you asked me that, I had just put the phone on mute for a second since I had to take a pain pill because of severe pain. This is weird that you know this!" She kept asking me how I knew.

"I'll tell you, but just let me ask a few questions. Can you rate your pain for me on a scale from zero to ten?"

"It's a seven, and this pain pill won't kick in for another thirty minutes. I'm in pain all the time." She told me she had numbness in her body, her legs and her arms. She also felt a buzzing sensation that had been going on for two weeks, 24/7. She described it like the vibrate setting on a phone, but throughout her whole body all the time.

"I couldn't have known that you were dealing with any of this. Do you mind if I try something?" I asked. She agreed. "In Jesus' name, I command all the pain in your body to leave. I command this infirmity to go," I said. "Now check your body to see what's happening."

"You know," she hesitated, "I do feel better. I feel the pain starting to go."

"What level is the pain at now?"

"I'd give it maybe a four."

"Okay," I said, "if the pain can go from a seven to a four, it can go all the way to zero. Is it okay if I pray one more time with you?"

"Yes, sure!"

I prayed again, commanding the pain and infirmity to leave her body. This time the pain went down to a two.

"This is amazing!" she said.

I asked her if we could pray again. This time she said it went down to a one, with just a slight ache. I asked, "Could I pray one more time, and then you tell me what happens in your body?" I prayed another short prayer.

"The buzzing just stopped in the upper part of my body!" she exclaimed. "It's completely gone!" The pain disappearing had gotten her attention, but when the buzzing left, it really caught her by surprise. She did not know what to do or how to respond. "I can't believe this is happening," she told me.

I continued, "If the Lord can do that in the upper part of your body, it can happen in the lower part of your body." We prayed again, and the buzzing in the lower part of her body stopped, and all the numbness left.

"I only have a small ache left in my legs," she said with shock. "I've been mad at God, wondering why He put this condition on me. People have told me maybe God did this to help me understand what other people are going through."

"If God wanted you to suffer from this disease, then the pain and buzzing wouldn't have stopped when I prayed. God didn't put this on you," I said. "He never puts sickness or disease on a person. Do you know the Lord's Prayer? It says, 'Our Father who art in heaven, hallowed be Your name. Your Kingdom come, Your will be done on earth as it is in heaven.' Is your disease or any other sickness in heaven?"

"No," she said.

"Right. And Jesus told us to pray for what is in heaven to be on earth. Your condition is not from Jesus. This is an attack from the evil one. Do you have a relationship with Jesus? Have you asked Him into your heart?"

"Oh yes, I have. I used to be a meth addict and dealer for years. My life was going nowhere, and I wanted to stop. I cried out to God, *You're going to have to help me. I can't do this.*"

She told me she had fallen down on the ground on her face back then and asked God for help. The next day when she woke up, a long-standing addiction was broken. She had seen God move in her life years ago in a powerful way. But somehow, she had started to believe that her disease was from God, so it confused her and made her frustrated and angry. She went on to explain all the debilitating things that had happened from it. She started opening up about her life, and we ended up talking on the phone for literally an hour. She told me she could not walk without using a walker or cane. She kept describing how her knees would buckle, how she was bruised all over, and that she had to take a ton of medications. She also had a rare blood disease and trembled like an eighty-year-old woman.

"But when you prayed," she explained, "the pain started to go, and the buzzing completely left. I've actually been pacing back and forth in my corridor, with my headset on, since you prayed for me. I could only walk six feet before, and then my knees would buckle or my legs would get too weak, and I'd have to grab on to something. I just realized I've been walking for 45 minutes as we've been talking. I can't do this—yet I'm walking without a cane!" She kept reiterating that it was impossible. She started opening up even more about all the things that were going on in her life and about how it had been hard on her relationship with her husband.

I then started to pray for her again, saying, "I break the spirit that is over you and over your husband." The phone call dropped right at that second. *That's pretty interesting*, I thought. I did not have a way to call her back.

About five minutes later, however, my phone rang. It was the same woman. She kept thanking me for praying. She could not believe what had happened to her. I prayed with her again and encouraged her not to let offense or anger step into her heart.

Here is the ironic thing: Her husband works with her, so he could see everything that was happening during our call. Every once in a while, I could overhear her telling him what was going on. She explained that at first, he was shaking his head when she was talking about her conditions with me. I told her she could just explain to him that she had not brought them up, Jesus had.

As we were ready to hang up, I told her, "This was the love of Jesus. He wanted you to know that He has heard your pain, your frustration and your cries. He wants you to know He did not put this sickness on you."

"I think you're right," she agreed. "This was an attack from the enemy."

"I'm believing for your complete healing," I told her. "If you can go from a level seven of constant pain that pain pills don't even stop, if the numbness in your body just left, and if the constant 24/7 head-to-toe buzzing is now gone, and on top of that you have been walking for 45 minutes without the aid of a cane, I would say

Jesus is healing your body!" It was awesome being part of what God was doing to transform this woman's life.

On another very ordinary day when I was doing my ordinary work in my ordinary room, I got a very ordinary phone call. It was a sales call from a travel company wanting my business. Normally, I would just say "I'm not interested" and end the call, but this day I had a faint, fleeting thought—so faint I could have dismissed it. But I know this is often how the Holy Spirit speaks, and that our job as believers is always to be looking and listening for His whisper and then responding to it, stepping out into risk in order to display the love and power of a good God.

Because of that, I thought I would at least listen to the sales guy's pitch and at the same time be listening for what the Holy Spirit might be doing. The caller, Luke, was fun and engaging. In the end, I purchased something from him because it was actually a good deal, and Jeanine and I had been looking for something similar. Luke then asked if I had any other questions before he transferred me to the verification process. This was the moment I could choose to respond by partnering with Jesus or not.

I chose to respond. "Luke," I said, "I actually do have a question. This may sound a bit odd or out there, but I have this gift of having pictures and impressions for people about what's going on with them. It's usually about physical issues they're dealing with. I'm not a psychic, and I'm not 100 percent right. I have often missed it. With that being said, would you like me to share the impressions I felt for you?"

Luke said, "Sure! I'm open to this kind of stuff. Shoot!"

I described three areas that I sensed were giving him issues.

"Man, that's crazy!" Luke said. "How did you know? Two of those happened last night, and I slept hardly at all because of the pain. The other condition I've had for twenty years, from an accident."

I had not named his specific diagnosis, but I had described all three of his issues perfectly, including where he experienced pain.

"Luke, describe your pain level if we were using a measuring scale of zero to ten," I said.

"I have a very high pain tolerance because I've had to learn to live with the pain for twenty years. For most people, the pain level would feel much higher, but I would say it's a four right now for me. And it often goes higher."

"So you've been in pain for twenty years, every day, without a break?"

"Yes, I just have to live with it."

I boldly said, "What if I told you I could get rid of your pain right now over the phone? What would you say about that?" I did not know for certain that Jesus was going to heal Luke; I just knew I wanted to respond to whatever it was God was doing. I trusted the results to Jesus.

Of course, this intrigued Luke. He was tired of living in pain. "I'm open. Go for it. Let's see what you got."

"Okay," I said. "Here is what's going to happen, Luke. In just a minute, all the pain will leave completely. Are you ready?"

"Yep. Go for it."

"Jesus, thank You for Your healing presence," I prayed. "I command all the pain associated with Luke's condition to go right now, in Jesus' name." Then I told Luke, "You're going to feel a warm sensation come into your back. . . ."

Before I could even finish, he said, "Oh, this is crazy! I can feel that!"

"Move your body around and look for the pain," I instructed.

"I can't feel the pain!" He was undone.

"That's awesome," I said, "but really look for the pain. Move, stretch, do whatever you need to do in order to find it."

"I can't find any pain!" Luke said. "And this heat on my back feels like Icy Hot."

"Luke, as you can tell, I'm a Christian, a follower of Jesus," I said. "Here's what I mean: I know there's so much baggage with 'religion,' but this has nothing to do with rules, regulations or religion. It's about a personal relationship with Jesus. I'm talking about God reaching out in His love and pursuing you with relationship. I don't know where your faith is, but today you encountered Jesus, and He's inviting you into relationship with Him. He knew about the conditions in your body; you tangibly felt Him and twenty years of pain left. What do you think about that?"

"This is amazing! I'm freaking out! Blown away! But to be honest," he said, "I've fallen away from faith. I went through a bad divorce, and I have all this anger in me."

"Luke, Jesus has never walked away from you. And He's not condemning you for walking away from Him. He's simply expressing that He's here, and He wants to bring you healing and have a relationship with you. There's no better time to be with Jesus than in the midst of your own pain, fear and brokenness. We don't get cleaned up and then come to Jesus. We come to Jesus as we are—broken and lost. He pours out His grace and love on us. I don't know your whole situation with your divorce, but I know you don't want to live in that anger. You need the grace of God to empower you to forgive, and to be healed. So my question is, Luke, are you ready to give your life fully to Jesus?"

With the sound of sniffles in my ear, I heard Luke say, "Yes, I'm ready."

I led Luke into praying with me, and it was so heartfelt. After he invited Jesus to be the Lord of his life, I said, "Luke, I'm going to pray for you right now, for the Holy Spirit to come tangibly over you and give you confidence and faith that you are fully accepted and loved." As I prayed that, Luke said he felt heat envelop his whole body and permeate all through him.

"Luke, the Holy Spirit is the Comforter. I think He's here to let you know that you've been accepted and loved back into relationship with Him."

"I gotta go now," he told me. "I gotta cry. This is unbelievable."

"Yeah, isn't this cool? You got a sale. I got a vacation. You got healed from twenty years of pain, and you gave your life to Jesus! I'd say that's a pretty good deal, huh?"

"That's a great deal." Luke chuckled as we got off the phone.

The Holy Spirit is working all the time, constantly whispering to us, inviting us to partner with Him to display the love and power of Jesus to broken, hurting, lost people. I was just sitting at my house minding my own business when I got a sales call. I was about ready to hang up, but I felt that slight impression from the Holy Spirit—such a fleeting thought that I could have missed it. But instead, I engaged and went with the slight whisper, and a sales call turned into a Kingdom encounter where a twenty-year condition was healed and a man committed his life to Jesus.

It is not enough just to look and listen for God's activity in the lives of people around us. We also have the opportunity to respond and partner with Him in that activity. When we simply respond to what Jesus is saying, we trust Him with the results. Success is in the obedience, not in the outcome. The outcome is up to Jesus. All we have to do is look, listen and respond.

S-T-O-P

Have you ever had one of those days where you felt discouraged? I have. I have found that we will have both discouraging days and good days. On those discouraging days, is the Kingdom still at hand? The question we have to ask ourselves is this: *Is this discouragement (or whatever we are facing, whether an internal or external situation) bigger than the present reality of the Kingdom?*

It may feel as though the things we face are bigger, but the truth is that the Kingdom is always at hand. Our job is simply to look, listen and respond to the reality of God's Kingdom, meaning His rule and reign. We have to remember that we are all in the process of renewing our minds, and we are also at war with an enemy who will always try to distort both the image of the Father and our image.

When we find ourselves entangled in the foggy gloom of discouragement, we need to look, listen and respond to the good news of the Gospel. I can tell you from experience that when you are in a funk, looking, listening and responding will feel like a battle, because it is. The voice of discouragement often comes packing with its buddies of condemnation and accusation. They come like charging pit bulls, trying to sink their teeth of hopelessness into your mind and emotions. When they bite down, their crushing jaws take hold, and like pit bulls, they don't want to let go. The "what-ifs," the "I should haves" or "I could haves" sink you deeper into despair. Their one job is to suffocate, mutilate and kill. These pit bulls of doubt are what the Bible calls vain imaginations or fiery darts of the evil one. They are doing their best to exalt themselves above the knowledge of God and convince you that you have no power. They puff themselves up, trying to make their image bigger than a good God, and they tell you that you have no choice but to bow in defeat and be conformed to their image.

The truth is that we are in Christ and Christ is in us—*even on bad days*. So when these vain imaginations come, 2 Corinthians 10:5 tells us that we are to cast them down and make them obedient to Christ. If we are told to cast them down, that means we have the power to do so in Christ. James 4:7 instructs us to submit to God and resist the enemy, and he will flee. *Submit* means to give over, or yield, to the power or authority of another. Instead of submitting to a lie that appears greater than the truth, we are to yield to the power and truth of the Gospel—Christ in us, the hope of glory (see Colossians 1:27). Whom the Son sets free is free indeed (see John 8:36). No longer do I live, but Christ lives in me. The life I now live, I live by faith (trust) in the Son of God (see Galatians 2:20). "Trust in the LORD with all your heart and lean not on your own understanding; in all your ways submit to him, and he will make your paths straight" (Proverbs 3:5–6). We put our confidence in God's Word and Spirit.

I once heard the Lord say to me, *When you're in the octagon of battle, just stop.* I saw a stop sign in my mind in the form of an octagon. Then the letters *S-T-O-P* popped out, and these words came:

S—Start
T—Thinking
O—On
P—Papa

So *S-T-O-P* giving attention to the lies, and *Start Thinking On Papa*. This is what Jesus did when He was tempted in the desert. In the thick of battle He set His thoughts on, and entrusted Himself to, the Father.

I have found that the Lord often whispers to us in those moments of battle, and our job is simply to look to Him, listen for His whisper and respond, no matter how we think and feel. In those moments, we must refuse to allow the bullying voice of the enemy to beat us down. Instead, we must focus on submitting and yielding to the voice of God.

7

CREATED TO DO GOOD WORKS

In Genesis 1 and 2, we see God creating all things. At the end of each day of creation, He said that what He created was "good." But after creating mankind in His image, He looked upon us and said it was "very good." We are God's very good creation. As bearers of His image, we are His handiwork, reflecting His image and goodness to the world around us. As He breathed life into us, He breathed His goodness into us, which is meant to flow through us into a hurting world.

When God created humanity, He told Adam and Eve, "Be fruitful and multiply; fill the earth and subdue it" (Genesis 1:28 NKJV). Part of that fruitfulness and multiplication also has to do with multiplying His good deeds and filling the earth with His goodness. Part of our commission from the very beginning was to fill the earth with the expression of our good God. This is our identity as His image bearers. We were created to do good works. He designed us to be co-laborers with Him and demonstrate His goodness throughout the earth.

Through the Fall, our identity and mission were distorted. Rather than subduing the earth with God's goodness, too often we have subdued the earth in war and strife. Instead of doing good works, we became something we were not created to be. We identified with the works of the evil one and became fruitful, multiplied and subdued the earth with evil, destruction and sin. Romans 5:12–21 explains that we were identified with Adam, but through Christ, God's abounding grace brings us back into our righteous identity in Christ:

> Therefore, just as sin entered the world through one man, and death through sin, and in this way death came to all people, because all sinned—
>
> To be sure, sin was in the world before the law was given, but sin is not charged against anyone's account where there is no law. Nevertheless, death reigned from the time of Adam to the time of Moses, even over those who did not sin by breaking a command, as did Adam, who is a pattern of the one to come.
>
> But the gift is not like the trespass. For if the many died by the trespass of the one man, how much more did God's grace and the gift that came by the grace of the one man, Jesus Christ, overflow to the many! Nor can the gift of God be compared with the result of one man's sin: The judgment followed one sin and brought condemnation, but the gift followed many trespasses and brought justification. For if, by the trespass of the one man, death reigned through that one man, how much more will those who receive God's abundant provision of grace and of the gift of righteousness reign in life through the one man, Jesus Christ!
>
> Consequently, just as one trespass resulted in condemnation for all people, so also one righteous act resulted in justification and life for all people. For just as through the disobedience of the one man the many were made sinners, so also through the obedience of the one man the many will be made righteous.
>
> The law was brought in so that the trespass might increase. But where sin increased, grace increased all the more, so that, just as sin

reigned in death, so also grace might reign through righteousness to bring eternal life through Jesus Christ our Lord.

It is through Jesus' redemptive grace that we have been given a new nature. We are no longer slaves to sin; we are alive in Christ (see Romans 6:6–8). His righteousness is our righteousness, and His goodness becomes our goodness.

We were in Jesus before we were in Adam. And through Jesus, we have a way back to the Father and back to His original design for our lives. We are defined by God's image, not by our sinful nature. In Christ, we are once again reconciled back to our intended identity as God's image bearers who reflect His goodness back into the earth. We can walk in that commission to do good works, be fruitful, multiply and subdue the earth with goodness as we reflect His image and put Jesus on display.

When God created the first man, Adam, He invited Adam to partner with Him in the process of accomplishing good works. Genesis 2:19–20 (ESV) tells us,

> Now out of the ground the LORD God had formed every beast of the field and every bird of the heavens and brought them to the man to see what he would call them. And whatever the man called every living creature, that was its name. The man gave names to all livestock and to the birds of the heavens and to every beast of the field.

God could have named the animals Himself, but He chose to bring Adam into the process. He partnered with Adam to accomplish His good works. The invitation is available to us as well. God has things He wants to accomplish on the earth, and He is inviting us to partner with Him in those endeavors.

Ephesians 2:10 tells us, "For we are God's handiwork, created in Christ Jesus to do good works, which God prepared in advance for us to do." God has already prepared good works ahead of time for you to do. They are not in your plans, but they are in His plans. What would happen if you woke up every day believing and expecting to step into a good work God had already prepared for you to do?

A good work could be healing the sick. It could be delivering someone from a demon. It could be you and your kids passing out a bag full of Big Macs to people. When we start our day with the knowledge that God has already stacked the deck with good works prepared in advance for us to do, we can have confidence that He has already laid the way for us. We can live each day with an expectation of how He may step in unexpectedly.

In Acts 10:38, we see "how God anointed Jesus of Nazareth with the Holy Spirit and power, and how he went around doing good and healing all who were under the power of the devil, because God was with him." Jesus' life was characterized by doing good and healing all who were oppressed. For Jesus, doing good sometimes looked like delivering someone from a demon. Sometimes it looked like extending forgiveness to a woman caught in adultery. Sometimes it looked like having dinner with sinners and tax collectors.

Jesus was constantly engaging in good works. We are invited to do the same. Everybody can do a good work God has prepared in advance. Good works come in many shapes and sizes. The common factor is that God has prepared them for us. It is what we were created for! All we have to do is join Him in them.

My wife and I were enjoying an afternoon date out for tea, one of Jeanine's favorite outings. But after I drink tea, I always need to use the restroom. As I got up from our table and walked toward it, a woman reached out toward me. With an intense look in her eye, she urgently said, "Do you remember me?"

In my mind, I was trying to place the woman and see if I could remember her. "No, I don't think I remember you," I replied with curiosity.

"I remember you! It was years ago, but I remember you. I didn't look like this then. I was all crippled up. Do you remember me?"

I was just beginning to pull up the memory from years before as she continued, "I was alone outside a store. My hands and feet were turned in on themselves from my disease. My husband had just abandoned me, and I didn't have anywhere to go. I was crying out for help, and no one was stopping for me. Then you came out of the store and stopped."

By now, I could exactly recall the incident she was referring to. It took me a minute because the woman in front of me did not look like the woman in my memory. I remember her being confined to a wheelchair. She had been beaten and bruised. As we talked more, we realized it must have been almost two decades earlier. She reminded me how I had given her money and told me she had used that money to call a cab and get into a hotel. I had prayed for her, including praying for her healing.

"Look at what I can do," she said as she extended her hands. "Remember how my hands were crippled before? They straightened after you prayed that night. And look at this," she said as she stood up out of her mechanical scooter and quickly spun around the room. She used the scooter now because of occasional seizures, but she said she had been healed from the crippling condition that had plagued her when we first met.

The woman, her current husband, Jeanine and I sat at a table for the next hour or so, catching up. She had brought a craft kit to work on while she enjoyed tea with her husband, and as we talked, she made a beautiful gift for Jeanine with hands that years ago could hardly hold the money I had handed her. We were amazed. She also told us about her current medical problems, including seizures and hearing issues. One of her ears was deaf from scar tissue and surgeries she had had as a child. No remaining eardrum or bones were inside, so her hearing was completely gone in that ear. As we talked, she asked if we could pray that her deaf ear might open.

As Jeanine and I prayed for her, she said she felt warmth and tingling first. Then she felt as though someone was putting things in place in her ear. It felt as though something was being built inside it, and as she felt it, she realized she was beginning to hear. She could feel the resonation and vibration in her ear.

"Then all of a sudden, *boom*, my ear opened!" she exclaimed. As we left, she said, "God healed me, and He always will be healing me!"

You never know what good work God has prepared for you to do. I had no idea so many years earlier that God had a good work prepared for me as I walked out of a store and saw a hurting woman. And I did not expect the good work that would happen so many years later, when Jeanine and I headed out for tea that day. It was just a good work God had already prepared in advance for us to do.

Wrong Turn? Or Right Turn?

Dave & Buster's arcade is a favorite family outing in the Blount household. With our large family, we love going on half-price Wednesdays. One cold Wednesday evening, we loaded up all the kids into the van and headed to the arcade for an evening of noise and fun. Jeanine and I were enjoying a relaxing conversation during the drive on the way there, and I guess I was really into our talk, because I drove right past my exit off the highway. Jeanine casually pointed it out and said we could just backtrack at the next exit. We started talking again, and I realized I missed the next exit, too. By the time we were off the highway, we were a couple of miles out of the way.

By now, the kids were getting anxious and asking when we would get to Dave & Buster's. I told them we would be there soon, but it was taking longer than we expected. I pulled up to the next intersection and saw a huge traffic backup.

"Well, looks like it will take even longer, kids. Sorry about that," I said to the sad faces behind me. We were stuck at a light, and it did not look as though we would be able to get through it soon.

"Hey, did you see that?" my wife blurted out.

"What?"

"That woman! Do you see that woman? Across the street, in that parking lot."

I looked to where Jeanine was pointing, and a moment later I saw what looked like an older lady shuffling in her pajamas across the parking lot. She had a sack from the fast-food restaurant down the street in her hand. It was way too cold outside for anyone to be walking far, especially dressed as she was.

"She fell and just now got up," Jeanine said. "Do you think she's all right?"

Suddenly, the woman fell over again. She slowly raised herself back up onto her feet and continued shuffling to the curb. To our horror, we realized she was going to try to cross the street. I immediately maneuvered the van over to a lane where we could get to her. We held our breath as we saw her shuffling across the street and again falling to the ground. Most people did not even seem to notice the poor lady trying to walk across the street, and the ones who did honked at her to get out of the way.

I finally managed to get our van through the intersection, and I pulled up beside the woman, who had by now made it across the street and into the adjoining parking lot. I rolled down the window and said, "Ma'am, I saw that you fell. Do you need any help?"

She mumbled something as she kept her eyes on the ground. I could not tell if she was physically ill, mentally ill or on something. Alzheimer's, maybe? It did not matter to me; I just wanted her to feel safe.

"Look, this is my wife, Jeanine." Jeanine smiled and waved. "And these are our kids." By then my kids had realized what was happening and switched their disappointment at the delay for family fun night into the compassion to help someone in need. They all sweetly said hello and waved. We were all trying to make the woman feel as unthreatened as possible, but she continued to mumble unintelligibly.

"Are you hurt?" I asked, to which I got a head shake that looked like a no.

"Where are you going?" I asked her.

"Home," she said. This was the first word we understood.

"Where is home? Is it far?"

She started pointing in the general direction, and we could see there were no houses or apartments nearby, so "home" could not have been too close.

"Could we give you a ride home, please?"

Immediately, the kids went into action. Ashley, our littlest daughter, eagerly offered to sit on the floor to make a seat available for the woman. They all put on big smiles and said, "Yes, let us give you a ride. You can sit right here!"

Jeanine stepped out of the car to steady the woman's arm so she would not fall again. We eventually coaxed her gently into the open seat and hoped she would be able to point us in the right direction. She did not say much, but we were able to make out her finger gestures and eventually find a small apartment building about half a mile away.

Jeanine and I stepped out of the car and asked the kids to stay put for a few minutes while we helped the woman inside. Before we even noticed, she had started shuffling up the entry steps and immediately fell onto the stairs. Jeanine and I helped her to her feet and picked up her food. We helped her slowly to her door. She fumbled through her pockets to find her keys. Unsteady hands attempted to unlock the door, and then the keys fell to the floor. I picked them up and opened the door.

"Is it okay if we make sure you get in all right?" I asked. We made sure she got safely into her small efficiency apartment, and we set her food out on the table. We were immediately struck by the scarcity of the apartment, and she obviously lived alone. This brought up a new concern—that perhaps no one was watching out for her safety. After all, she had just walked a mile in freezing temperatures to get a fast-food dinner.

"Do you mind if we come check on you again?" I asked. Somehow, we managed to get her phone number and address. We offered to input our contact information into her phone, and we showed her how to call us. We urged her to call if she ever needed food, instead of walking across the busy street herself, but we were unsure how much she understood.

The next day, Jeanine brought a couple of sacks of groceries with essentials like fruit, milk, bread and sandwich meat to her. We had no idea if she would remember or recognize us, so we felt it best that Jeanine go alone. That way, having an unknown man at her door would not scare the woman. Over the next few months, Jeanine continued to stop by occasionally to make sure she was safe and fed. After she had visited a few times, she could tell the house was being cleaned and groceries were being brought in, so she stopped going since the woman seemed wary of her presence.

Wrong place, wrong time? Or right place, right time? I believe those two wrong turns took us down the right turns to get us exactly where God wanted us to be at that very moment. He had prepared the good work for us to do in advance.

So often, we let unexpected turns frustrate us—whether it is literally a missed turn in traffic or an unexpected turn in life. We can shift our mindset, however, to realizing that God could be orchestrating those unexpected turns to put us in His right place at His right time—landing us squarely inside the good work He created in advance for us to do.

Cravings and Crutches

I am often amazed at the lengths God will go to in getting us in front of the people He wants us to minister to. Jeanine and I try to take each of our kids out for one-on-one special times together. I was on a dude date with our then nine-year-old son, Tyler, to two of his favorite places. We were on a trip to the mall to go to the LEGO store and Auntie Anne's pretzels.

After Tyler got his LEGO fix, we headed over to sink our teeth into a delicious cinnamon pretzel, only to find out the shop was closed due to a flood in the store. Bummed that we could not get a pretzel, I suggested we go to another mall across town, to the other Auntie Anne's pretzel place. Tyler's eyes lit up as he said, "Really? You'd take me to the other mall?"

"Yeah, let's go."

We got to the other mall twenty minutes away, and when we walked in, I saw a teenage boy on crutches. I immediately began to wonder if God had set this situation up to get us to this mall at this time. Was this a good work God had created for us to do? I thought to myself, *Let's get our Auntie Anne's pretzels, and then we'll see about praying for the young man.*

We got our hot, fresh cinnamon pretzels and rounded the corner, only to find that the teen and his family were gone. Disappointed, I started heading toward the exit when I saw him heading out of the mall with his family. I thought, *If they stop or if we catch up to them, I'll see if they'll let us pray for him.*

Sure enough, just in that very instant, the family suddenly stopped. Tyler and I walked right over to them. Tyler is always on board for praying for people!

I asked, "Hey, what happened to you?"

"I injured my ankle at a game," he replied.

"Are you in a lot of pain?"

"Yes. I can't move it or put any weight on it."

I turned toward the young man's dad and said, "We love to pray for people, and we've seen Jesus heal a lot of people when we pray. Would it be okay if I prayed for your son?" He nodded yes, so I asked the young man, "Is that okay with you as well?"

He looked at me and then looked at his dad, who gave him the safe nod of approval. Then I asked him on a scale of zero to ten what his pain level was, and he said it was about a seven.

"Can we put our hands on your shoulder and pray?" I asked.

He agreed, so there we were, with our cinnamon pretzels in one hand and our other hand on this teenage boy. Tyler and I started to pray a simple, quick prayer: "Jesus, let Your power come upon his ankle. Pain, go." Then I explained to him, "Sometimes when we pray for people, they start to feel heat and tingling, or the pain just leaves. Are you feeling anything right now?"

"I'm feeling a tingling in my ankle right now."

"Did you feel that before we started praying?"

He said he had not. I continued to pray, blessing the presence of God on him. Then I invited him to try to do something he could not do before. He started moving his ankle around, surprising himself.

"I couldn't do that before!" he said.

I asked him what his pain level was, and he said it was about a three now. "If your pain can go from a seven to a three, then it can go from a three to a zero," I told him.

With a shocked look, he said okay, so Tyler and I prayed again. This time, the young man started moving his ankle around even more. He cautiously put all his weight on that foot, and then he started walking normally, with his crutches in his hand.

"There's no more pain!" he said excitedly.

I said excitedly, "Isn't Jesus awesome?"

The young man and his family agreed, "Yes, He is!"

Tyler and I walked out of the mall, thanking Jesus for healing the kid and for our freshly baked cinnamon pretzels. As we got into our van to drive off, we watched the teen walking normally to his family's car, with his crutches in hand, smiling in wonder. We were also smiling in wonder, because we knew that only God could have orchestrated that encounter.

God chose us as the means through which He would do His good works. We need a realization that we carry His presence wherever we go. We are the Church, the Body of Christ. We walk into places as the hands and feet of Jesus. You and I are Jesus with skin on to the people around us. The Kingdom of God is going to come through His Church, because that is how He set it up. But we have to step out and be who we were created to be. God has already said yes to us; we just have to say yes to Him. We just have to take a little step, and He goes the extra mile.

An Unforgotten Woman

Late one night I was on my way home from a service at church, and I called a friend who lives on the East Coast. When he answered, I kept on hearing *beep, beep, beep* in the background. I asked, "Hey, are you at a grocery store?" He said yes, he was. All of a sudden, I received an impression that I felt was a word of knowledge I could not have known on my own. I did not have time to think before it came out of my mouth: "Is there a short, dark-skinned lady a little over five feet tall standing in line in front of you?"

He said, "Yeah. What do you have for her?" He sounded a little shocked, but not that surprised. He and I had often pressed in to hear the Lord for others while we were on the phone with each other. We had seen two or three people healed that way. But nonetheless, I was taken aback.

Bewildered, I said, "I don't have anything. I just saw a short, dark-skinned lady in front of you. There really is a lady like that in front of you?" As I said this, I started getting a shooting pain in my lower back, going down into my hips. I recognized this as a word of knowledge that God wanted to heal her. I told my friend I thought there was something wrong with her back, going down into her hips.

The thing I love about this friend is his boldness and his intense desire to press into the Kingdom. He was on the other side of the country and had no insight from God about this woman. I was in the comfort and anonymity of my van in Oklahoma City, while he was smack-dab in the line of fire, right where he would risk looking foolish and embarrassed if he shared the impression and I had missed it.

Because of his passion and desire to see the Kingdom of God released, though, my friend stepped out boldly. Over the phone I heard this: "Excuse me, ma'am. I'd like to share something with you. . . ."

A loud commotion suddenly started, and I heard a woman emphatically telling my friend that she did *not* want to hear anything he had to tell her. I heard another man join in the ruckus, and then the phone call dropped.

I thought, *Oh no! Did I just get my friend in a fight? This must not be God, because there's conflict.* Then I remembered that there is always conflict when the Kingdom of God is advancing. After a few minutes I was able to call him back, and I still heard the commotion in the background. "Dude! Are you okay?"

I heard my friend saying, "Listen, ma'am. I'm a Christian—"

She interrupted him, shouting, *"I'll have none of that!"* Then she added, still loudly, "I was a preacher's daughter, and if you want to go toe-to-toe, we can!"

I overheard him as he explained, "I don't want to argue. I was just minding my own business on the phone with my friend when the Lord described you in detail to him. He said there's something wrong with your back, going down into your hips."

I heard the other man's voice yelling in the background, "There's *nothing* wrong with her back!"

But the lady went silent for the first time since the scene began. After a pause, she said, "Something *is* wrong with my back and hips. Let me talk to your friend."

He handed her the phone, and to be honest, I was freaked out. I was in Oklahoma City, and they were on the East Coast at a grocery checkout at 11:00 p.m. I started expecting that God would give me a download of prophetic information for this woman and it would be amazing. But I did not receive anything. I just explained to her the impression I had about her pain and where it was. All I felt led to say to her was that God loved her. He had not forsaken her. He was near to her. He knew her situation. He had not forgotten her.

She started weeping. *"Oh, Jesus! Oh, Jesus!"*

I just kept telling her how much God loved her.

She finally said, "You don't understand. My husband died recently, and we have several children. I thought God had left me. I thought He had abandoned me. I was a preacher's daughter, so I know better, but why did God take my husband away from me?"

She began pouring out her life to me. The pain in her back was so severe she thought it was literally going to kill her. I just kept telling her how much God loved her.

"I'm just some guy in Oklahoma City, but God loves you so much that He would speak to me while you are in a grocery store on the other side of the country to tell you that He is near and that He hasn't forgotten you."

I got off the phone with her, and she continued talking to my friend. He prayed for her back, and she experienced healing from the pain. She told him how much this experience would change her life. She had been in such despair over her husband's death that she was ready to commit suicide. She had been tired of living, until this happened. She continued to call my friend for a few days afterward, telling him that she could not believe how God had come near to her.

God knew this woman's struggles, and He was not about to give up on her, even if she wanted to give up on Him. He will go so far to show His goodness that He will take one man in Oklahoma, another man on the other side of the country, line up their schedules so that they call each other late at night, and interrupt their conversation to tell them about a woman He wants to touch. He wanted this woman to know that she was not forsaken, and He prepared a good work for my friend and me in advance to make sure she knew that. He has good works already prepared so He can demonstrate His love. All we have to do is step into what He already created us to do and put Jesus on display.

Jesus Calls the Most Unlikely

In John 4:1–42, we find a treasure in the story of the woman at the well. Through this story, we learn that God calls the most unlikely people, regardless of their race, gender, class, social status, or past or present circumstances. No human construct or experience can strip you of your identity as one created in God's image to do good works in His Kingdom.

In this story, Jesus and the disciples are traveling from Judah in the south to Galilee in the north. Their long journey takes them through Samaria, a region devout Jews often avoided because of long-standing ethnic and religious disparities. The Jews often reviled the Samaritans as half-breeds who had diluted and perverted their religion into something unrecognizable and unholy. When Jesus and the disciples became tired and hungry, however, Jesus rested by Jacob's well while the disciples went into the nearby town for food. A Samaritan woman approached the well to draw water. This was during the heat of the day, when only a social outcast would come to the well. Rather than ignoring her, as any righteous Jew—especially a rabbi—would do, Jesus actually spoke to her. Not only did He speak to her, He asked her for a drink of water.

Our 21st-century Western interpretive lenses don't fully grasp what Jesus was doing here. Women, especially Samaritan women, were considered unclean. For Jesus to drink from her bucket would be to defile Himself and make Himself unclean. In other words, Jesus was saying He was willing to make Himself unclean just to have a conversation with her. He was giving her dignity, value and worth when she expected at the least to be ignored, and at the most to be hated, rejected or harmed.

Jesus tells her that He has living water, and that anyone who drinks this water will never thirst again. He then shares words of knowledge about her life that He only could have known through supernatural revelation. He tells her she has had five husbands, and that the man she now lives with is not her husband. He knows her history but does not condemn, judge or ignore her. Nor does He condone her lifestyle. When He shares these words with her, it opens her heart to have a religious conversation about God, worship and truth.

Again, Jesus was breaking every possible taboo. Not only was He speaking with a Samaritan, He was also discussing deep theological issues with an *uneducated*, *sinful woman*—and any one of those three words would have kept any decent rabbi from entering into such a conversation. It was a real, honest conversation in which she asked questions and He challenged her assumptions. In other words, He talked with her as though she was a real person whose questions and thoughts were valid, important and worthy of a response. Jesus looked past her ethnicity, gender, history, social status and sins, and He saw right to the person in front of Him, who needed living water more than she could fathom. He saw through all the societal barriers, to a woman who needed what only He had, and He was willing to break through all those barriers to offer her what she really needed—Himself, the living water.

The woman then recognized that He was the Messiah. Her encounter with Jesus had reshaped the way she viewed herself and her past. His love captivated and emboldened her to go into a village in which she had been looked down on and shamed. As she drank from the living water and His perfect love, it cast out any fear and shame and lifted her head so that she proclaimed this good news: "Come, see a man who told me everything I ever did" (John 4:29). She shared about Jesus with everyone there, and as a result, many believed. They asked Jesus to spend time with them, and He ended up staying for two days.

While this is the longest one-on-one conversation recorded in the Bible between Jesus and any single person, Christian tradition fills in the gaps in the rest of her story. History tells us she went on to be baptized among the first Christians at Pentecost. At her baptism she was given the name *Photini*, meaning "enlightened one," because her encounter with Christ had enlightened her. Despite being a woman and a Samaritan and having an offensive past, tradition tells us she became a leader and a missionary in Carthage, North Africa, where she preached the Gospel. She was considered one of the greatest evangelists, rivaling even the apostles.

Tradition goes on to say that while in Carthage, Photini had a dream that she would travel to Rome to confront Nero, the evil emperor who was torturing and killing Christians. This once shameful woman, who would avoid other people by going to get water in the heat of the day, was now emboldened to the point of being willing to stand up to the most powerful man in the world. She reportedly had a chance to confront Nero with the truth of the Gospel, and as a result, she was beaten and imprisoned. While in prison, she converted the emperor's daughter and her household to faith in Christ. Further infuriated, Nero continued to torture Photini and eventually killed her by throwing her down a dry well.

This Samaritan woman, who once was as dry as the well into which she was thrown, became a testimony of living water through her life and martyrdom. Her life is so honored that Orthodox Christians consider her a saint equal to the apostles. This is the esteemed legacy of the sinful Samaritan woman at the well.

Photini's story tells us that none of us are disqualified. A woman of the wrong ethnicity, with a scandalous past, she was the most unlikely person to encounter Jesus and be used by Him. No obstacles can keep us from Jesus' love and commissioning. None of us are excluded, regardless of our past, race, gender, status or age. What Photini did not know was that she had been created to do good works and put Jesus on display.

I saw Jesus choosing the most unlikely people on one of my trips to South Africa. We came into an obscure village where a pastor had been doing a weekly outreach to the community. The village was mainly made up of women, a few older men and some children. As we walked in, we could hear the rumbling of surprised conversation in another language as they caught sight of us. The pastor just turned to us and said, "They want to know why you would come to a place like this, when there are so many bigger places you could go. We are the least of the least. Nobody comes here."

I replied, "All the more reason we would come here. This is where Jesus would come. I'm honored to be here."

During a service at the church, I had a word of knowledge for healing of pain in the lower right back and hip. To my astonishment, about twenty women all responded as having that particular condition. Rather than trying to pray for all of them, I instructed them how to pray for each other. I coached the first person in praying for the second. "As freely as you have received, freely give," I said as I had the woman who had just been healed turn to pray for the next woman. As each woman was healed, she prayed for the next. All I did was coach and encourage them. Every one of the twenty women was completely healed of her back and hip pain.

"You women are now the ministry team," I said. I sent them out in the church to pray for everyone who needed healing. Healings were breaking out all across the church.

The pastor did an altar call at the end and asked who would like to receive Jesus as Savior for the first time. I was shocked to see that the twenty women raised their hands. God had been using them powerfully, and they were not even believers before that evening!

After the pastor led them in a prayer for salvation, I said, "Though you feel as if you are the most unlikely people, God is commissioning you to go into your village, share your testimony, heal the sick just as you did here tonight, and lead people to Jesus, just as you were led to Christ."

The next day, I was in a meeting with a bunch of pastors from the surrounding region. The pastor who did outreach in that village was sharing testimonies from what had happened the day before. He said that ever since then, his phone had been blowing up with messages from the women in the village. They had been going out into the village and seeing incredible testimonies of healings and salvations.

Then he came up to me and said, "Can I ask you a theological question? This baffles my mind. Not one of those women who were praying for each other was saved, and healings were still breaking out. One of the ladies is a known prostitute. Another is a witch doctor. How can that be?"

"You didn't tell me one was a prostitute and another a witch doctor. But honestly, even if I had known that, it wouldn't have changed how I did anything. The only thing that comes to my mind is Acts 2:17. Jesus said He would pour out His Spirit on *all* flesh, not just Christian flesh. *All* flesh. So, remember what happened to the twenty women?"

"They all gave their lives to Jesus. And they've all been sharing their testimony since," he confirmed.

"Then does it really matter whom God chooses to pour His Spirit on?" I said. "Jesus will use the most unlikely—even rejected women from a rejected village."

Women and People 50+

Several years ago, the Lord gave me a prophetic word that He told me to share everywhere I speak. Wherever I have shared this message, I have seen the Holy Spirit break out and empower people. This is what He said: *Brian, I'm going to pour My Spirit out on women and those in their fifties and above like never before. Some of the greatest evangelists, pastors, teachers and miracle workers we will see will be women and those 50+.*

If you are a woman or are in the 50+ age group, I have good news for you: God especially wants to use you to put Jesus on display with love and power. I believe God is highlighting these two groups because they are two demographics the enemy has tried to silence. The Church has partnered with lies that have kept these groups silent, and God is changing that.

If you are a woman, too often both the enemy and the Church have told you that because you are female, you don't have a voice and a commissioning. That is a fabrication. Jesus' presence is on you. Parts of the Church have put their thumb on you and said you cannot speak, or you can only do certain things. Those things are untrue. In Christ, there is no male or female. The first evangelists you see in the Bible were all women. Mary Magdalene and Mary of Bethany were the first to be witnesses of Jesus' resurrection and to spread the Good News (see Matthew 28:1–8). Saint Photini not only led her entire Samaritan town to faith but also became a missionary to Carthage and Rome. Jesus loves to empower women, and women are among the best at bringing others to Jesus.

If you are a man or woman age 50+, I am sorry you have been told that when you get to a certain age, there is no part for you to play. You have too often been excluded or devalued. You have so much faith, wisdom and history with God that you bring to the table when you are putting Jesus on display with love and power. You are valuable and needed, and the best years are ahead of you. God is still beginning a new thing in you. As you catch on fire, I guarantee that the youth and young adults will see that and flock to you as never before.

Some of my favorite testimonies have come from women and from people 50 and above. One woman named Kerri, who is also 50+, went with me on a trip to South Africa. In her everyday life at home, she is an IT manager at a large corporation. She is pretty quiet and reserved, but she has a deep love, confidence and boldness in Jesus and a great desire for people to experience Jesus.

While we were in South Africa, she was at a grocery store with another 50+ South African lady named Joke. As they were checking out, they asked the cashier if she needed prayer for anything, if she had any pain. They took a huge step of risk. To their amazement, the woman not only wanted prayer, but was also instantly healed from leg and back pain as they prayed. Joke told the cashier, "Jesus loves you. Tell others it was Jesus who healed you." After that, the attendant who'd been working alongside her asked for prayer, too. This second woman was also healed. Next, those two women asked if Kerri and Joke could pray for a few more people, and they opened up a small room where Kerri and Joke could pray more privately.

Soon word spread through the store that God was healing people. Just when Kerri thought they were done praying for people, they opened the door to see a long line of women waiting for prayer. That small risk of praying for the first cashier had opened the door for so many people to experience the power and presence of God. By the end of it all, twenty women had experienced healing and heard the good news that this was Jesus showing His love for them. Joke also asked each woman if Jesus lived in her heart and instructed her that she could pray in the same manner for her family and friends for Jesus to heal them. Not only were these two women praying, they were also equipping the women in how to pray for each other. The presence of God became so thick in the room that when one woman merely walked in, she was instantly healed.

The funny thing is that some men from our group had tried praying for people in that same grocery store just moments earlier and had been kicked out. Something about these two women was unthreatening, safe and unassuming. They were able to minister because of the very assets that the enemy tries to use to keep them quiet. This all happened because two women, who were also 50+, just happened to believe that Jesus could use them to pray for a cashier.

I want to end this chapter by praying an impartation and commissioning over you if you are a woman and/or are someone in the 50+ age group. Right now, I want to break off every lie of the enemy over you if you are in one or both of those groups.

God, You have created this person with a purpose and destiny. You have commissioned him or her with the good news of the Gospel. Lord, pour out fresh anointing and fresh commissioning on this person.

And regardless of age, gender, race, ethnicity, education, status or history, I commission this person to stand in his or her identity as a beloved son or daughter, created in Your image to do Your good works.

I commission this reader now to heal the sick, preach the Gospel, raise the dead, do all the works of the Kingdom and destroy the works of the evil one. As freely as I have received, I freely give away.

You were created to do good works. Now may you go and put Jesus on display with love and power.

8

EMPOWERED BY LOVE

When Jesus was baptized, the Spirit descended on Him in the form of a dove, and the Father spoke from heaven: "This is my Son, whom I love; with him I am well pleased" (Matthew 3:17). It was this act that gave Jesus what He needed to step into ministry. He was empowered by the Spirit and by the love of the Father. And He shows us that same love so that we can be empowered by it, too.

Jesus was commonly referred to as being a friend of sinners when He showed that love. This was not meant as a compliment; it was a scandalous accusation. Mark 2:16–17 tells us,

> When the teachers of the law who were Pharisees saw him eating with the sinners and tax collectors, they asked his disciples: "Why does he eat with tax collectors and sinners?"
>
> On hearing this, Jesus said to them, "It is not the healthy who need a doctor, but the sick. I have not come to call the righteous, but sinners."

In the Pharisees' minds, they were the important ones. They were the ones who had kept God's laws, studied the Scriptures, prayed and made the appropriate sacrifices. They were offended that Jesus chose to spend His time with heathens. He was with prostitutes, adulterers and tax collectors. Tax collectors were not only considered thieves for skimming extra taxes to line their own pockets; they were also considered political traitors who were supporting the Roman occupation. The Pharisees were astounded that these were the people Jesus was spending His time with.

The Scandalous Table of Fellowship

Not only was Jesus spending time with these people, He was eating with them. In the culture of the time, eating with people meant more than just sharing food. It meant declaring a covenant relationship with them, committing to love and serve them. People were very careful about whom they shared a table with, and Jesus had chosen a scandalous table of fellowship filled with the rejects of society, just as He had done with the woman at the well.

Jesus still chooses a scandalous table of fellowship. I believe if Jesus were here today, He would be going to all the disgraceful places to seek out sinners and find the lost. He would visit all the shameful places many Christians feel are beneath them. He would scour the places many Christians think are too filthy to go to. He would be recklessly, lavishly, excessively scandalous.

Not only that, but Jesus also invited people of various views, experiences and backgrounds to His table. You can see this paradox within His disciples. Among the Twelve were a tax collector, a religious zealot and uneducated fishermen. A zealot who was trying to destroy Rome sat alongside a tax collector who was raising taxes to support Rome. These people would never have eaten together, except for one reason: Jesus. Because of Jesus, they all had something to unite around. They could all lay down their personal agendas to fellowship with Him and His friends. All were welcome at this table, and all could find love and acceptance there.

Reckless Love

The Pharisees did not get it. They could not understand why Jesus would choose to spend His time with sinners, and they hated Him for it. Luke 15:1–2 tells us, "Now the tax collectors and sinners were all gathering around to hear Jesus. But the Pharisees and the teachers of the law muttered, 'This man welcomes sinners and eats with them.'"

In response to this accusation, Jesus tells three parables we call the "lost parables"—the stories of the lost sheep, the lost coin and the lost (prodigal) son. This trilogy in Luke 15 describes the lengths to which God will go to rescue the lost and bring them into His care. These three parables sum up why Jesus chose to spend His time with tax collectors and sinners, and they confront the religious mindset that casts away sinful people.

Have you ever lost something valuable such as your wallet, your keys or your wedding ring? Or that holy grail, your phone? You will go to any length to find the missing object. Everything stops; nobody moves or does anything else until you find it. This is the heart of Jesus for every lost person. Love compels Him to search lost people out and do whatever it takes to find them. I think Cory Asbury's song "Reckless Love" says it all, where he talks about how the reckless love of God chases us down until He finds us, no matter what.

In the first lost parable of the sheep and the shepherd, the shepherd leaves 99 sheep behind to search for the one that is missing. Searching all through the open country, he goes to incredible lengths to find that lost sheep. Eventually, upon finding it, he places it over his shoulders in love, carries it back home and throws a party with his friends to celebrate the found sheep. We find similar imagery in Ezekiel 34:11–16:

> I myself will search for my sheep and look after them. As a shepherd looks after his scattered flock when he is with them, so will

I look after my sheep. I will rescue them from all the places where they were scattered on a day of clouds and darkness. . . . I myself will tend my sheep and have them lie down, declares the Sovereign LORD. I will search for the lost and bring back the strays. I will bind up the injured and strengthen the weak.

This is the Father's heart for us, and it is also His heart for every lost person. The second lost parable Jesus tells demonstrates this even more. A woman has ten coins, and she loses one of them. She searches her house frantically, using the broom to sweep her entire home until she finds it. She is so overwhelmed with excitement at finding the coin that she throws a party for all her neighbors to come celebrate with her. This does not make any sense. Why spend more money on a party than the coin was probably worth in the first place to celebrate it being found? It is lavish, excessive and irrational. But that is exactly what God's love is like. His love for the lost is over-the-top.

The third lost parable is about the prodigal son who leaves his father's home, takes his share of the inheritance and squanders it on a sinful lifestyle. After sinking to the point of starvation, he finds himself eating the slop that only pigs would eat. He finally hits rock bottom, remembers the bountiful table at his father's house and decides to make the long journey back home, with his head held down in shame. He hopes only to be a servant in his father's house, where he once stood as a son. As he stumbles toward home, he sees his father watching him from afar, and he is paralyzed by guilt and fear, knowing that he does not even deserve to be a servant because of his rebelliousness and reckless living. But he is astonished by what he sees—his father running toward him with tears rolling down his cheeks and his arms open wide, yelling, "My son! My son! You've come home!" The father lavishes him with love, putting a ring and the best robe on him. With a joyful cry of celebration, he tells the servants to bring his finest, fattest calf. "We must celebrate! My son was lost, but now he's found." Then the father throws an epic party for his beloved prodigal son.

Did you notice that all these parables end with a party? God is overjoyed at every lost son who returns, and He celebrates each one's homecoming. Every life is valuable. Every life deserves celebration and excessive love.

This is the heart of the Father for us, and it is His heart for all who don't yet know His loving embrace. As His children, we also are to have this heart for the lost. As ones who walk in His image, we are to be shepherds who stop at no length to search for the lost sheep. We are to be the woman who scours her home to find the coin and who lavishly celebrates when it is found. We are to be the father who runs toward the returning lost son. The Father's love empowers us with that same love to seek and save the lost.

Going after the One

I love what Heidi Baker says: "Stop for the one." Stop for the one person in front of you. Stop for the one you see. Each of the "lost parables" in Luke 15 involves going after the one. The father went after the one lost son. The woman searched for the one lost coin. The shepherd left 99 sheep behind to find the one lost sheep.

We never know what chain of events will follow because we stopped for the one. We may never know the results of praying for someone, or engaging with a person in an encouraging conversation, or even just smiling at someone.

My friend Gordon is an excellent example of this. He loves going after the one, even if it may be embarrassing or requires persistence and going out of the way for that person to encounter the love of God. My favorite story out of Gordon's many testimonies involves his going to a crowded restaurant for a business lunch. Gordon is the owner of a tech company, and he was having lunch with Paul, a manager for one of his suppliers, so they were there to talk business. The two men noticed another man, however, who was shuffling slowly into the restaurant. He was hunched over nearly 90 degrees, and he dragged his leg behind him. Gordon could tell he was in tremendous pain and assumed that his back was the problem. Gordon knew that Paul was a Christian, too, but he was not sure how Paul felt about healing or miracles. He said to Paul, "I'm going to go pray for that guy." Paul stared at him in disbelief. "Yeah," Gordon continued, "I see all kinds of healings, and I expect Jesus to heal him right now."

Paul was a little wary and unsure of how to pray for someone's healing, but he did want to be part of what God was doing. Gordon suggested that Paul could simply place his hand on the man's shoulder and pray in agreement with what Gordon would pray. They both approached the man, who was sitting at his table, waiting for his food.

"Hi, my name is Gordon, and I love to pray for people. Can I pray for your back? I believe Jesus is going to heal you right now."

The man looked up with anger in his eyes. "It's not my back; it's my foot. It was mangled in an accident years ago. I couldn't afford to have surgery, so everything healed all broken."

When he said that, Gordon and Paul looked down and saw that his foot was bent at a 45-degree angle from his leg. The lower part of his leg looked as if it had been snapped and had healed that way.

Gordon continued, "I believe if you let me pray for you, Jesus will heal you right now."

"You bunch of hypocrites!" the man blurted. "I used to be part of a large denomination, but now I'm a deist. You guys don't practice what you preach." He continued his rant for several minutes.

"Well, I believe Jesus will heal a deist, too," Gordon explained. "Let me pray for you."

"If you believe in that stuff, then sure, you can pray for me."

"I'd like to pray for you right here, right now," Gordon said.

The man looked at him like a deer caught in the headlights. "You're kidding!"

"No, I'd really like to pray for you. I believe Jesus will heal you," Gordon said. Paul was giving him sideways glances, wondering how far he was going to push it.

"All right, if you insist," the man conceded.

Gordon was hoping the man would shift his chair around to expose his leg so he could lay hands on the ankle, but he did not. Instead, Gordon actually crawled underneath the table to place his hands on the spot and began praying.

By this time, the situation was awkward. Gordon was under the table, Paul did not know what to do, and other people in the crowded restaurant were giving them strange looks. Gordon popped up from under the table and said, "Now get up and walk."

"You really expect me to be healed, don't you?" the man asked skeptically.

"Yeah, I do."

The man got up, and all of a sudden his eyes got really big. Then Gordon and Paul's eyes got big, too. Something had clearly changed.

"Now let's walk," Gordon said.

Sometimes working a healing miracle like this requires encouragement. In Scripture, you see others lifting people up to walk, leading them and picking them up. Gordon and the deist started walking from one end of the restaurant to the other. The man was standing up almost completely upright and walking straight. Gordon looked down at the man's foot and saw that it, too, was almost straight. The man looked at him in shocked disbelief.

They walked back to the table, and Gordon asked the man how his pain was. It had been at a level ten out of ten when he had come into the restaurant, and now he said it was at a three.

"I haven't felt this good since I had my accident over a decade ago," the man told Gordon and Paul. The presence of God was really strong in the room. He sat down, dumbfounded.

"Jesus is healing you right now," Gordon explained to the man. "Let's pray again." This time the man turned his chair around so Gordon could have access to his injury without crawling underneath the table. Gordon laid hands on the spot, and this time Paul also put his hand on the man's shoulder. There was a whole shift in the environment. Skepticism and anger had been replaced by faith and love. The presence of God brought peace and comfort. It was almost as though everything around them stood still. People were watching and looking, unsure what was happening. But it was clear to everyone that something was happening.

Gordon prayed again, thanking Jesus for bringing the pain from a ten to a three. "I command all the pain to go to a zero now, in the name of Jesus. I command full range of motion and activity in this leg and foot," Gordon prayed. "Okay, check it again."

The man jumped up, walking from one end of the restaurant to the other, completely healed. His leg was straight, and his back was straight. He became a different person, going from the angry, bitter man who had first walked in to someone who had encountered the healing love of God.

"You know what?" Gordon said. "Jesus healing you is His invitation, calling you back into relationship with Him. How do you want to respond?"

"I'm in. Let's do it."

The fruit of Gordon stopping for the one was unimaginable. A man was healed and set free from years of crippling pain, and his heart was opened up to the power of the Gospel. He gave his heart to Jesus.

Another time, I was with Gordon and a group of friends in a large city in South Africa. We had just finished a lunch together in which we had seen God heal several restaurant staff, and they had opened their hearts to Jesus. We were then walking back to our bed-and-breakfast, strolling through the center of town. I noticed three guys standing around. At first, I felt a pull to stop and pray for them, but to be honest, I was tired and just wanted to get some rest. We kept on walking.

After a moment, I realized Gordon was no longer with us. I turned around to see that he had stopped for one of the three guys I had just passed by. We saw him praying, and then we heard the man shouting with excitement as he was healed—the same man I had just walked past. He and his two friends told Gordon that they were already believers, but that this encounter with God had increased their faith.

Next thing we knew, Gordon was praying for the two other guys. We all decided to go over and see what God was doing. What happened next was something none of us could believe. Gordon had simply stopped for this one man, and something broke open. The Kingdom of God engulfed the entire area where we were all standing. Gordon introduced us to the three men, and then out of nowhere people started coming toward us out of stores and restaurants, and people on the sidewalk stopped to see what was going on. We all started clueing in that God was drawing people to us, and each of us found ourselves praying for them. Healings were breaking out, and people were coming to Christ.

A Hindu woman and her young son walked up to my friend Blaine, and she asked if he would like to buy some stickers. She was selling them to get food for herself and her son, who was sick and running a fever.

"I would be happy to buy some stickers," Blaine said. "How much are they?" She told him the price, and he said, "No, I mean how much to buy all your stickers?"

She was taken back. "You want to buy *all* the stickers?" she asked.

Blaine reached into his wallet and took out more money than she had asked for. Through tears of thankfulness, she handed Blaine the stickers.

"Now that I've bought your stickers, I would like to give them back to you as a gift so you can make more money for you and your son," Blaine said. "Before you go, let's get your little boy healed." Blaine prayed for the boy, and his fever broke right then. He was completely healed.

The woman was blown away by the love and generosity Blaine had shown her. He explained to her, "It was Jesus who healed your son and impressed on my heart to buy all your stickers. Would you and your son like to give your hearts to Jesus?"

Her words in response were priceless: "Why wouldn't we want to give our lives to Jesus?" Blaine then prayed with them to receive Christ.

I looked up to see my friends Phill and Dan praying for people, and even more of them were getting healed and opening their hearts to Jesus. I looked over and asked a man I saw what he needed prayer for. He said his lower back really hurt. We were standing next to a fast-food restaurant that had outdoor seating. I grabbed a chair and asked the guy to take a seat. It felt as though one of his legs was shorter than the other, so I had him sit back so I could look at them. Sure enough, one leg was a couple of inches shorter.

I stooped down in front of him, holding his feet in my hands, about ready to pray, when a store manager came out of the nearby supermarket. "What's going on?" he asked as he saw the gathering crowd where we were praying for people.

I told the manager, "This man has been having horrible back pain, and one of his legs is shorter than the other. I'm going to pray for him, and Jesus is going to heal him."

The manager looked skeptical, but before he could say anything else, the shorter leg grew out and the guy himself started freaking out as he felt it growing. The manager could not believe what he was seeing. The guy in the chair stood up and began moving and bending. He could not find the pain he had felt for years.

I was not sure what the manager was thinking as he witnessed all of this happening. But the next thing I knew, he said to me, "Do you think God would heal my back?"

"Absolutely," I told him.

He explained that it would be a miracle if he was healed. He had had several back surgeries and was always in pain. He also had limited range of motion in his back. I suggested he take a seat so we could see if he had a shorter leg, too, and he said he knew one of his legs was shorter than the other because a doctor had told him that already.

As I prayed for him, we were both stunned. Not only did his shorter leg grow out, but it also kept growing—about two inches farther than his longer leg! The man looked up at me as if to say, "What did you just do?!"

I just smiled and jokingly said, "You want to be taller, right? Don't worry! The Holy Spirit is just readjusting your spine." Then I spoke to the leg to go back, and it did. I spoke to his normal leg to grow out more, and sure enough, it grew out just as far as the other one had before it had gone back into place.

I said, "Sir, this is just a sign to make you wonder how real God is and that He is healing your back." Then I prayed again, telling the longer leg to go back into place. The man was shaking his head, dumbfounded by what he was seeing and feeling as his legs grew in and out.

Next, I asked him to stand and move his back around to see if he could do something he could not do before. Tears of joy filled his eyes as he bent over so far that he could touch the ground with the palms of his hands. He sprang back up and said, "I can't believe it! There's no more pain! It's all gone. Listen, can you heal my boss's back, too?"

"No, I can't. But I believe Jesus can," I said.

"His back is even worse than mine. He has metal in his back and is on medication for the pain. He can't bend over at all. Can you wait here just a minute?"

He came back a few minutes later with his boss. By this time, my friends Dan, Phill and Blaine had joined me. "Just let these guys pray for you," the manager encouraged his boss. "Sit down, and he will grow out your legs and heal your back."

The look on the boss's face was hysterical as he processed through what his manager was saying. You could tell he was wondering if the man was nuts, but he could not deny the testimony of his friend. He could tell that his friend had been healed and was able to move in ways he could not have before, so he finally decided to let us pray for him. What had happened to his friend was now happening to him—both his legs grew in and out as we prayed for him. Then all his pain left.

Phill asked the man about the metal in his back. He said, "I have two rods, and I'm in chronic pain. It always feels tight; I can't even bend down anymore."

"Brian and I see people with metal in their bodies regain full range of motion all the time," Phill told him, "and all their pain leaves, too. Can we pray for your spine to be completely healed, all your stiffness and pain to go and full flexibility to return?"

"Sure, go for it," the boss said cynically.

As we prayed for him, he said his back got really hot. Then he said all the pain was gone! He bent over and moved in ways that should have been medically impossible with rods in his back. He was beyond shocked.

While that was happening, the store manager ran across the street and grabbed his wife and four other people to come receive prayer. Blaine, Phill and Dan began to minister to his wife and friends, while Gordon was off praying for other people. One lady was in pain all over due to cancer. As Blaine prayed for her, she experienced deliverance and all the pain left her body.

I headed back toward the restaurant to return the chair I had borrowed, where I met three young ladies who worked there standing outside. They had been watching everything that had been happening on the street. I told them I had borrowed their chair and asked if they needed prayer for anything. All three said yes. One of the girls was healed from a back issue she had had for several years. Each of them felt the tangible presence of God so strongly that I had to hold one of them up to prevent her from falling over. All of them opened their hearts to receive Jesus.

We did not move more than thirty feet in an hour and a half. We saw well over thirty people get radically touched by the Holy Spirit during that time. Before we left, the manager of the nearby grocery store came up to me and asked if we could come back the next morning. He offered to open up his store for us to pray for anyone who wanted prayer. A couple of us did go back the next morning and were able to pray with several employees. Again, we saw the Kingdom break in with healings, along with people opening their hearts to Jesus.

All of this happened because my friend Gordon decided to stop for the one I had passed by. You never know what will happen from just stopping for the one.

Follow the Way of Love

Jesus had more than a healing ministry. He had more than a deliverance ministry. Jesus had a people ministry. He would stop for the one in front of Him to put the love of the Father on display. All healings, deliverances from demons, resurrections, signs and wonders were like hugs and kisses from a good God to the battered and broken ones standing before Jesus. He ministered to the whole person—spirit, soul and body. His ministry took on various forms. Depending on people's needs, it might mean healing, deliverance from demons, multiplying food for the masses, forgiving sins or stretching out His arms on Calvary to embrace a prodigal world.

Likewise, our goal is not healing or any other specific manifestation or form of ministry. Rather, our goal is simply to put Jesus on display, as He put the Father on display to the one in front of Him. Each manifestation of His Spirit was like an individually wrapped gift Jesus gave that went far beyond meeting the person's immediate need. These tangible gifts were empowered by love, penetrating deep into people's hearts and showing them their value, worth and identity.

Jesus is still handing out empowered gifts of love to His Church. These empowered gifts of love are listed in 1 Corinthians 12:8–10: words of knowledge, words of wisdom, faith, healing, miracles, prophecy, distinguishing between spirits, speaking in tongues and interpretation of tongues. While 1 Corinthians 12 and 14 focus more on the spiritual gifts, chapter 13 focuses on the motivation behind those spiritual gifts—love. Operating in spiritual gifts is never to be a substitute for love. Rather, we are to operate in spiritual gifts as an expression of love. Without love, we have nothing to offer at all. First Corinthians 13:1–3 states it this way:

> If I speak in the tongues of men or of angels, but do not have love, I am only a resounding gong or a clanging cymbal. If I have the gift of prophecy and can fathom all mysteries and all knowledge, and if I have a faith that can move mountains, but do not have love, I am nothing. If I give all I possess to the poor and give over my body to hardship that I may boast, but do not have love, I gain nothing.

Love must be the motivation for all we do in ministering to others. People are not a notch in our belt. People are not a testimony for us to share. People are not evidence of how spiritual or gifted or pleasing to God we are. People are not to be used to prove to ourselves that we are worthy, loved or needed. People are the focal point of God's love and desire. For us to treat them as anything less than that is to use them for our own benefit and not to the glory of God.

Our primary goal in ministering to others is to show them how much God loves them. Whether they are healed or not, whether they experience breakthrough or not, they should always leave a conversation with us feeling more loved by God and more loved by us. How we treat people matters very much to Jesus. Our motivating factor and primary goal must always be love.

Putting Jesus on display not only involves things like healing the sick, and signs and wonders; it also means loving your spouse, your kids and others. It means feeding the poor and clothing the naked. As John 13:35 tells us, "By this everyone will know that you are my disciples, if you love one another." The Kingdom is not just found in the marvelous; it is found in the mundane, day-to-day walking out of this life in a posture of love. It is cultivating and putting into practice the fruit and the gifts of the Spirit.

Our spiritual gifts are most effective when they grow alongside the fruit of the Spirit: love, joy, peace, patience, kindness, goodness, faithfulness, gentleness and self-control (see Galatians 5:22–23). We cultivate the fruit of the Spirit and put into practice His gifts in order to put Jesus on display.

First Corinthians 14:1 admonishes us, "Follow the way of love and eagerly desire gifts of the Spirit." Loving people and growing in spiritual gifts are not competing or contradictory aspects of God's heart. They are two sides of the same coin. We are encouraged in this passage to do both. Follow love! That is of primary importance. But to neglect eagerly desiring spiritual gifts is also a way of neglecting growing in love, because one of the ways God shows His love to us is through the operation of gifts such as healing, prophecy, miracles, words of knowledge and faith. As we follow the way of love, we must also eagerly desire spiritual gifts.

What does it mean to eagerly desire something? I often feel an eager desire for chips and queso. My kids have eager desires every year around Christmas and their birthdays. We eagerly desire all kinds of things—relationships, growth, safety or the newest iPhone or iPad. But we are told to eagerly desire spiritual gifts, and that is only a self-serving or selfish desire if our motivation is something other than love for others. Love for others can motivate us to eagerly desire growing in spiritual gifts, because ministering in spiritual gifts is a way to express God's love to people in an incredibly effective way.

Spiritual gifts are tools. As with any tool, these can be used for good or harm. We have all seen examples of people with tremendous spiritual gifting who also do tremendous spiritual harm. That does not disqualify the need for the gift. It only repudiates the improper motivation behind the use of the gift. As we follow the way of love, spiritual gifts can help us in that primary goal of showing people the love of God. Follow the way of love, *and* eagerly desire spiritual gifts. The goal should be to cultivate both the fruit of the Spirit and the power of the Spirit.

The Generosity of God

I was in a restaurant in South Africa with the pastor of the church where we were ministering. Her name was Arianne, and her husband, Ian, and my friend Blaine Cook were also with us. The four of us were trying to have a nice, quiet dinner, but we were being interrupted by commotion from a large group of women nearby. This group around a table close to us was celebrating a birthday, and the shouts, laughs and drinks were all flowing. We were having a hard time hearing each other at our table because of it, and I could tell I was becoming irritated. Then I heard the still, small voice in my heart: *I want you to pay for their dinner.*

Really, God? Over time, I have learned that oftentimes the things that irritate us are invitations from God to be empowered by love and show forth the generosity of His heart. But to be honest, this time I thought to myself, *Let me find out how much it will cost first*. The truth is, love and generosity will always cost you something.

I motioned our waitress over and asked her to find out how much the bill would be for the table with the party. When she asked why, I said that I wanted to pay their bill, but I did not want them to know I was the one paying. Love for this rowdy group of women was growing in my heart, and I knew this was Jesus. The waitress was shocked that I wanted to pay their bill.

My friend Blaine noticed my conversation with the waitress. "Are you paying their bill? If that's what you're doing, I want in on that, too," Blaine said as he reached into his wallet and handed me a handful of cash. Blaine is one of the most generous people I know. He has learned over a lifetime that you cannot outgive God and that generosity has a way of opening people's hearts like nothing else, as well as opening our hearts toward them. A friend once said that one of the best ways to show love and reach the hearts of people is by sending out little green missionaries. These little green missionaries are called "cash money."

Then God hit my heart with compassion again, this time for the waitress. I sensed Him say, *Pay the whole bill yourself. Take the money that Blaine gave you and use that as a tip for the waitress, on top of what you were already going to tip.*

I again felt the empowering generosity of the Father nudging my heart. He wanted to bless not only these women but also the one standing right in front of me. When I handed her the cash, she began weeping as tears of joy ran down her face. Only God knew what she needed. The little green missionaries went to work. They opened the door to her heart, and we were able to minister to her. As a result, the Lord gave me a word of knowledge about a condition in her body, and she was healed and gave her heart to Jesus. We had no idea of the impact this simple act of generosity would have.

A few minutes later, I heard the ladies at the party table get uproariously louder. They had just gotten the news that their bill had been paid. The waitress must not have been able to keep the secret, because before we knew it, those ladies swarmed our table. They were over the top in thanking us.

"Why would you do that?" one of them asked.

We just kept replying, "We wanted to bless you because God loves you." It especially had impact in South Africa that a table of white people would pay for a table of black people. They were overwhelmed.

I started talking with the woman whose birthday was being celebrated. She was a Christian, and she started telling me the backstory behind the party. She had been trying to save money to start a business that would help serve impoverished kids in the area who could not get into school because of the expenses of supplies, uniforms and fees. In the middle of trying to save money, she felt as if she should invite all her friends out to dinner to celebrate her birthday. She knew it did not make any sense because she could not really afford to have a party at an expensive restaurant while she was saving money to start the business. But God had a plan. He knew that we would be at the restaurant at the same time, and He had a plan to pay the bill. As she talked about her business, I felt the Lord tell me to give the rest of what I had in my wallet to her. As I did that, another wave of love hit her. She dropped her face into her hands, shaking her head in disbelief as tears rolled down her cheeks and out through her fingers.

God's generosity opened a door for us to begin ministering to the women. God started giving us these empowered gifts of love in the form of words of knowledge, prophetic words and healing. As we were ministering, the power of God was hitting them. As I prayed for one lady, I had to catch her before she hit the floor as the power of God overcame her. I looked over to Blaine as he was ministering to a woman who had collapsed in his arms. She was weeping as Blaine was telling her the secrets of her heart. Arianne and Ian jumped right in along with us, praying for and loving on these women.

The next thing we knew, we saw the waitress marching out of the kitchen with several others from the kitchen crew and serving staff. "Can you pray for my friends, too?" she asked.

The power of God fell mightily on them as well. Generosity had opened up an outpouring of God's love in the center of this upscale restaurant, while other customers were staring at us between their bites of steak and sips of wine.

I had started the evening feeling frustrated. I had not had a generous heart. It was the overflow of God's love and generosity toward these women that moved my heart. He told me to be generous, and His love empowered me to do so. That act of love and generosity opened up heaven on that restaurant. That night, not only a full table of women and our waitress, but also a slew of kitchen crew and staff, were radically touched by God's love.

The Least of These

In Matthew 25:34–40, Jesus tells a parable about the King on the Day of Judgment who separates the sheep on His right from the goats on His left:

> Then the King will say to those on his right, "Come, you who are blessed by my Father; take your inheritance, the kingdom prepared for you since the creation of the world. For I was hungry and you gave me something to eat, I was thirsty and you gave me something to drink, I was a stranger and you invited me in, I needed clothes and you clothed me, I was sick and you looked after me, I was in prison and you came to visit me."
>
> Then the righteous will answer him, "Lord, when did we see you hungry and feed you, or thirsty and give you something to

drink? When did we see you a stranger and invite you in, or needing clothes and clothe you? When did we see you sick or in prison
and go to visit you?"

The King will reply, "Truly I tell you, whatever you did for one
of the least of these brothers and sisters of mine, you did for me."

Jesus cares about "the least of these," those who are the throw-
aways of society. The ones we would rather overlook are the very
ones His heart longs for. He cares about the hungry, orphaned,
imprisoned and needy. When we turn our eye away from them, we
are being like the Pharisees who don't understand Jesus' scandalous table of fellowship. When we do turn our attention, hearts
and actions toward them, we are partnering with the heart of
God as His love empowers us to put Jesus on display to these
people.

One of the churches we work with in South Africa has a weekly
street outreach in which the members take food to an impoverished
area of town where many homeless people live on the streets. Many
of the people they serve are victims of AIDS or other chronic and
terminal illnesses. It is a wonderful opportunity to follow the way
of love by showing God's many ways of healing through offering
food to eat, conversation, prayer and comfort. When I joined them
one evening, I was stunned to see the number of people huddled
together on the streets around makeshift fire pits or bundled under
plastic tarps or cardboard as protection from the wind and cold.
Some were shivering under whatever small bit of clothing or thin
blanket they could find.

That night, I spoke with a woman whose body was wracked
with tuberculosis and AIDS. There was no hope in her eyes. Her
face was weathered and wrinkled from pain and disappointment.
She was in tremendous pain all over, and my heart broke for her
as I handed her a cup of soup and some bread.

She said to me, "What do I have to live for? I'm just an old
woman now, dying in the street from AIDS. You see that man over

there? He's the one who gave me AIDS." She set the food down beside her as if to say, "It doesn't even matter if I eat."

I had no words for her, only compassion. Even if I did have words, that was not what she needed. What she needed was someone to show her dignity and love, and to hear her story. I simply grabbed her and held her as she wept, and I wept with her. In the embrace of that hug, I said, "Holy Spirit come. Touch this woman. Bring healing to her heart and body."

I have no idea if her AIDS was healed that night, but what I do know is that she experienced love. After my embrace with her, her weathered frown had turned into a beaming smile as she looked at me and said there was no more pain in her body and she was able to breathe freely. I could tell hope had entered into a hopeless place. She turned to the others around us and said, "Jesus touched me." She was smiling ear to ear as she picked up her meal and began to eat.

As we continued moving among the groups of people, offering them food and prayer, someone approached me and said, "Brian, you have to come pray for this guy. Something's wrong with him."

The man was lying under a piece of plastic held up by a stick to create a homemade tent. The people on the street told me that the man had not gotten out of the tent for about three weeks, and they feared he was dying soon. As I approached the tent, I heard a sound I know too well: the heavy breathing death rattle of someone who is close to death. The man was struggling to gasp every breath.

My immediate thought was, *I don't want this man to die alone.* I did not think about getting him healed. A prayer for a miracle did not even cross my mind. I just did not want him to die alone. I jumped into his tent because I thought he could die at any moment. The tent reeked of urine, sickness and death. At least someone would be with him as he died. That was my only thought—to bring comfort and God's presence to a dying man.

"Sir," I said, "you're not alone." I don't even know if he heard me or not. All the man could do was gasp for any bit of breath.

In the Kingdom of God, all ministry is of equal value. There is equal significance in raising someone from the dead and helping someone pass from this life to the next. The pay is the same. In that moment, as I embraced a dying man, I heard the Spirit whisper two things to me: *Brian, I want you to rebuke the spirit of infirmity, and release My peace.*

I prayed simply, "Holy Spirit, would You come? I release Your peace. I command the Spirit of peace to come, and I rebuke the spirit of infirmity."

The Spirit of peace fell so strongly that I thought the man had died. The horrible sounds stopped. The striving for breath ceased. Everything was completely still.

Then the man took a breath—a clear, normal breath. "I can breathe!" he said. "I can breathe!"

"Jesus just came into your tent and healed you, my friend. He loves you, and you're not alone," I said. The man wept in amazement. After a few moments, I asked him, "Do you want to try to get out of your tent?"

"I can't walk," he said.

"If you can breathe, you can walk," I told him as I helped him onto his feet and he ventured out of the tent for the first time in weeks.

Within minutes, this man was walking up and down the street, shouting, "Jesus is Lord! Jesus has healed me!" Every step he took was not only a testimony of God's healing power, but also a testimony to the huddled poor that Jesus had come to their place. Jesus was on their streets. Jesus cared about them. He was healing them in every way imaginable by feeding them, supporting them, comforting them, healing them from pain, listening to them and even rescuing someone from near death. Jesus used it all to His glory.

The "least of these" are not just found in Africa. They are right where you live, too. I got lost while driving one day. I had just prayed, *Lord, open my eyes to see, and open my heart to hear Your voice.* About thirty seconds later I saw a large, muscular man lying beside the road. I did not know if he was taking an unusual nap, suffering from heatstroke, or was drunk or dead. Two contradictory thoughts battled in my mind: *Keep driving,* and *Go see how you can help this man.*

I chose to follow the way of love and drove over toward him. I called out, "Sir! Sir!" over and over, getting louder each time. With no response, I literally thought he was dead.

Finally, he roused and blurted out, "What the ——— ?!" I guess he was not dead after all. He was definitely alive and had some colorful words to say about it.

I replied, "Sir, I just wanted to make sure you were okay." He went on creatively expressing his sentiments, and then he walked toward my car while reaching into his pocket.

A gun? A knife? I wondered. Suddenly I was not so sure about this.

"You got a cig, man?" he asked.

"No, sorry. Can I help you? Are you okay?" I asked.

"Here's a dollar. Can you get me some cigarettes?"

"Keep your dollar. Let me go get you some water, and I'll get some cigarettes. I'll be back."

"Yeah, I bet I'll never see you again."

I came back three minutes later with a pack of cigarettes, a lighter, water and a Gatorade. He looked a little stunned.

"What are you doing helping me? Do you know you could get killed in a place like this? What are you, some alien? Or a Jehovah's Witness?"

"No, I'm just a guy who saw a man in trouble and wanted to make sure you're okay. That's all. I'm a follower of Jesus, and He has shown His love to me, and to you, someone He created and loves."

"God doesn't love me! I've killed people! I was in the service, killing people for our country and for God. What are you saying? I could knock your teeth through the back of your head right now and kill you. Are you ready to die today?"

"If I have to, I guess I will, but I don't want to. I have a family. I believe God is with me and that I'll be okay. But even if not, I'm still safe with God," I said. "I'm not here to do anything else except help you in any way I can and love on you because God so loves you, Bro."

He laughed and slurred out more creative, colorful, poetic language. "You really believe this stuff!"

"Yeah, I really do."

"You're messed up, man." Then he began to ask me those unanswerable questions about life and God. Clearly, he was a deep thinker.

"I'm not sure about all that," I answered, "but I do know Jesus is the expressed revelation of the Father in heaven. Instead of punishing us, He was beaten, crucified and hung on a tree to wipe out all our sins in our past, present and future." In spite of his circumstances, I could tell by the nature of his questions that this guy was well-educated, so we were talking in some hefty theological terms.

"What are you saying? You're crazy!" he said. "Or maybe you're not. It's true, I did pray earlier today, *God, show me that You're real and You're here*." Again he asked me some hard, unanswerable questions as he was processing through the pain, tragedy, war and death in his life. "What do you know, anyway, pretty boy?" he finished with.

I smiled. "It's not about comparing. I've been through some rough times, though." I shared a little bit of my story, and he changed his demeanor somewhat.

"What are you doing helping me?" he asked again.

I kept responding, "You're worth it. God loves you. You're a big guy with a lot of pain, but with a soft, compassionate heart."

"You're out of your mind," he insisted. I could tell he was beginning to soften, but not too much. "Okay," he said, "if you're for real, could you take me somewhere I really need to go today?"

I said sure and let him into my car. As we drove across town, he continued with the questions, kept telling me how crazy I was and asked what I was doing with such a crazed person like him.

"I just want to show you that you're loved and created for a purpose, and you're valuable to God. I'm not earning anything by doing this. As freely as I received His love, I'm just simply freely giving it away."

As we pulled up to his destination, he looked at me, shaking his head. "I'm not sure why you did this. I could have killed you, but thank you."

"Can I pray for you?" I asked.

He grabbed my hand and said with complete sincerity, "Lord, please save me from the demons in my mind." I prayed for him, and then this big, tough man clasped my hand, kissed it and said, "Thanks for helping me."

As he got out of the car, I said, "Thanks for not killing me!"

He smiled and chuckled a bit as he turned and walked into the building. It was a place where he could get some help, and he walked in with hope in his eyes. I think he wanted to go to get sobered up and get his life on track.

God loves people. He loves sick people. He loves broken people. He loves dirty and smelly people. He loves addicted people. He loves vile and crude people. He loves religious people. He loves people who reject Him. He loves people who may never love Him back. Love is not just something God does. His very nature is love, and His love empowers us to live as Jesus lived and to love people, too. Empowered love looks like something—it looks like Jesus.

9

TREASURE IN
EARTHEN VESSELS

In 2 Corinthians 4:7 (NKJV), Paul refers to the Gospel as "treasure in earthen vessels." The Gospel is the glory and power of Christ. It is a treasure. But God has chosen to place this treasure inside jars of clay—us. We are frail, vulnerable and inadequate, but what we carry is of immense value. In Galatians 2:20, Paul tells us, "I have been crucified with Christ and I no longer live, but Christ lives in me. The life I now live in the body, I live by faith in the Son of God, who loved me and gave himself for me." The treasure transcends and overshadows the earthen vessel it inhabits. We don't have to be perfect to hold the treasure. In our mess, the message of the Gospel shines forth the most. Because we are earthen vessels, we will struggle, have hard days and feel weak, but we will still carry the glory of Christ within us.

I love the way *The Message* translates 2 Corinthians 4:7–12:

> If you only look at us, you might well miss the brightness. We carry this precious Message around in the unadorned clay pots of

our ordinary lives. That's to prevent anyone from confusing God's incomparable power with us. As it is, there's not much chance of that. You know for yourselves that we're not much to look at. We've been surrounded and battered by troubles, but we're not demoralized; we're not sure what to do, but we know that God knows what to do; we've been spiritually terrorized, but God hasn't left our side; we've been thrown down, but we haven't broken. What they did to Jesus, they do to us—trial and torture, mockery and murder; what Jesus did among them, he does in us—he lives! Our lives are at constant risk for Jesus' sake, which makes Jesus' life all the more evident in us. While we're going through the worst, you're getting in on the best!

It is our very weaknesses and the things that we feel disqualify us that actually make the Gospel message break through even more. Paul even says, "If I must boast, I will boast of the things that show my weakness" (2 Corinthians 11:30). In our weakness, God's power can come through. When we are broken, we are not destroyed, because the strong One is fighting for us. When we feel surrounded by death and heartache, the life of Jesus breaks through. We will ever be the earthen vessels that are weak, but the treasure we carry overcomes all our weakness.

Both Missionary and Mission Field

John Wimber used to say that we are both the missionary and the mission field. God works in us as He works through us. We will never be beyond needing His love, ministry and healing, but our need for those things should never deter us from the mission field of bringing that same healing to others.

My wife makes this brilliant statement: "God doesn't give His mission to the mature. He matures those on mission." When Jesus sent His disciples out on mission in Matthew 10:7–8, they were still very broken, confused people. Being sent out to minister to others in Matthew 10 happened before James and John fought over who was going to sit at Jesus' right hand and have prominence and power (see Matthew 20:20–23; Mark 10:35–40). It happened before Peter denied Jesus upon His arrest or attacked a man and cut off his ear (see Matthew 26:69–75; John 18:10–11). It even happened before any of the disciples acknowledged that Jesus was the Son of God (see Matthew 16:13–20). Clearly, Jesus was not using their right motives, good choices or even their correct theology of who He was as a prerequisite to sending them out to preach the message of the Kingdom, heal the sick, cast out demons and raise the dead.

Don't get me wrong; walking with Christ means becoming more like Him. But as my wife says, partnering with Jesus in His mission exposes our deficits and gives us an opportunity to grow. Jesus matures those on mission. Nothing quite exposes our hearts like dealing with failure, temptation, fear and the pain of rejection. Stepping out in the mission of Christ gives us opportunities to experience all those things, and they should push us further into Jesus rather than deterring us from continuing to engage in His mission.

Author and theologian Henri Nouwen popularized the phrase "wounded healer." In his book by that same title, he describes the brokenness of our world and the brokenness of the people who are called to bring healing to that world. Just because we are wounded does not mean we don't have something to offer. It is in our weakness that Jesus is made strong. Rather than allowing our woundedness to keep us from engaging in mission, our woundedness can be what presses us further into Jesus so that we can be more effective in ministering to others.

The Bible is full of examples of broken people whom God used tremendously. Among the heroes of the Bible are adulterers, murderers and thieves. We see Gideon, who battled insecurity and self-doubt. Jacob was so fearful that he manipulated his way through life to avoid pain and confrontation. Both Paul and Timothy struggled with physical illnesses that affected them. Jeremiah and Elijah battled severe depression.

I am not advocating brokenness, and I am certainly not excusing sin. But the fact remains that none of us are fully well, healed and without sin in this lifetime. All of us have things we struggle with. It is vitally important that we cooperate with the sanctifying work of the Spirit to heal us in those areas. Nonetheless, if we wait till we have everything together to join Jesus on His mission, we will always find a reason to disqualify ourselves.

Failure and Sin

What do you do with your failure, sin and poor choices? What do you do with those images that often suspend time, that play in slow motion like a car accident? Your life flashes before you. Fear grips you and strikes at the core of your being. This is often what happens with our failures. We relive those moments of failure, poor choices, sin and humanity. The suspended time lapse we live in swirls with questions: *Why did I do that? Why did I say that?* That suspension where we are trapped in the moment of our failure is haunting and paralyzing. It leads into a depression that shackles us to a hopeless despair. We mask it, and we try to hide the skeletons of failure. But the reality is that the haunting never goes away by masking it; it only collects more clutter. Like in a junk drawer, it is harder to find those valuables you have placed inside. When we don't deal with our failures, they become so magnified and overwhelming that we shut down, or we dump out everything in order to find what we are looking for.

The truth is that we all fail, sin and have a skeleton or two we are trying to hide. The more we hide, the greater the haunting. Dealing with our failure and sin requires us to recognize the mess, fall forward into God's arms of grace like the prodigal son and let the Father lavish His love and acceptance on us. We must learn to draw our identity not in our failures, sin or humanity, but in the destiny of His gaze and breath of life that comes when His Spirit speaks to the dry, dead bones of hopelessness and despair our failures and sin have produced. We know that the wages of our sin, failures and poor choices is death. We experience death at some level every time we fail, and we are all faced with the reality that death is coming, and it comes for all. What man sowed in his disobedience produced death, so death stalks us all. It is like a bloodhound tracking us down, like a criminal on the run.

We must learn to feast at the table of God's grace instead of feasting on our failures, sin and poor choices. We bring our failures to the foot of the cross, where a man who knew no failure, sin or poor choices embraced our punishment as though He deserved it. There, stripped naked, bloody and beaten beyond recognition, He cried out, "Forgive them, for they know not what they do" (Luke 23:34 NKJV). Mercy triumphed over judgment that day. The blood-hounds of hell became confused and whimpered away. Though death came, His life had been given, not taken. Jesus gave up His life so that the punishment of death was broken in His body, and life now flowed where He had been pierced. Because Jesus was forsaken, no one else would ever have to be. His death became our death, and His life our life. No longer do I live, but Christ lives in me. The life I now live, I live by faith in Him, not in myself.

So what do we do with our failures, sin and poor choices? We exchange our wages of sin for the currency of His grace and hope. That exchange does not come through prayer alone, but in a submitted life saturated in the awareness that every breath we breathe is a gift of grace. This great exchange is for all who have been feeding on the junk food of this life and are left emaciated and starving for the nutrients of heaven. We are invited to come to the table of grace and feast freely. We cannot buy our way out. We cannot climb our way out or hide. We can only come to His table and consume His body that was broken for us and drink from the life in His blood that was spilled out for us. Then the DNA of His life permeates through us—no longer the darkened imprisonment of failures, sin and poor choices. In this great exchange, we are offered life, and life more abundantly.

In short, we simply admit our need, and we consume His grace and don't stop consuming it. We delight in it rather than focusing on our failures, sin and poor choices. When we consume this grace, we, too, cry out, "Forgive them, for they know not what they do." God's gift of grace frees us to forgive ourselves and others—to grant relief from payment owed, and to cease feeling resentment against an offender. We pardon those (including ourselves) who have harmed us. Grace exchanges our failures, sin and poor choices for hope and life as we consume grace and cultivate forgiveness.

What will you do with your haunting failures, sins and poor choices? You have two tables to feed from: your failures or His grace. Death or life. Let's choose life and His grace.

Pain and Hopelessness

Maybe you are more spiritual than I am, but I still struggle with things, mainly depression. I am growing, and I am so much further than I used to be. But I still struggle daily with growing in Christ, conforming my thoughts to His, and overcoming lies I have believed about God, others and myself. I grew up in a fatherless home, and I was often shuffled between my mom, my grandparents and different friends. I was drinking regularly, smoking weed and huffing gas by the time I was eleven years old. I rarely attended school, and my time was more often spent walking the streets, getting into trouble and partying with my friends. I spent the next few years in and out of drug rehabs and boys' homes. In other words, I had a pretty unstable upbringing that left me with a lot of wounds and deficits.

The reason I share this is because I know how the enemy works. He is constantly trash-talking, and unfortunately, we still often buy into the trash he tries to feed us. We can either believe the trash talk the enemy is trying to feed us, or we can feed on the truth of the Good News, that Jesus is the way for the hopeless. I am a sucker for self-pity and for looking at my own pain from time to time. Let me say there is a time to press into your pain, but always with Jesus. It is also helpful to have a trusted friend or counselor to talk to, something I do weekly. For some people, internal pain or depression is chemically based. We would never fault someone who had diabetes for taking insulin. Nor should we look down on those who need medication for any such struggle. Depression can also have spiritual and emotional causes or factors, however, which can complicate the chemical issues.

Pain sucks. No one likes it, and we all try to avoid it at any cost. The problem is, we will never escape pain until the restoration of all things is fully manifested in Jesus. This is the hope we all have been given. Jesus is the hope of the world—even your internal world. I know what it is like to get sucked into the deceptive dialogue of the enemy and find myself wallowing in the dump of despair. The truth is, we are all wounded healers. We are growing in Christ. We all have pain and hardship, and we will all face trials, tribulations and loss. But we all must choose who is Lord: the pain, the struggles, the sickness or Jesus.

Sometimes I allow the pain to become more real than Jesus. But when I listen to His voice and look to Him, I see the pain in a different way. I see an opportunity to be a reflection of His hope and allow the pain not to rule, but to fuel a deep place of compassion and empathy for others. A wise friend once said feelings are great servants but horrible masters. The enemy always distorts and perverts God-given gifts so he can try to rule us. We all have feelings.

Don't ever ignore them, but never allow them to rule you. Embrace the pain and trust in Jesus. Never allow the pain to become lord.

Pray Like Never Before

The year 2013 was a time when I needed to pray for the sick like never before. It was by far the worst year of my life. My mom had been diagnosed with stage 4 melanoma cancer, and her odds of survival were slim. We started out that year with her surgery to try to remove the cancer, followed by extensive medical care. I was also experiencing some very odd physical problems myself—tremendous pain every time I ate, which at times kept me bedridden. I later found out I had an incredibly rare disease called achalasia, in which the esophagus stops working and food cannot pass into the stomach. Throughout this time, our then nine-year-old son Tyler was also experiencing a problem that would eventually grow into weeks of hospitalization and the torment of an undiagnosed and misdiagnosed mystery illness.

Tyler's struggles began with something that seemed simple: a constant burp. After a referral to a gastrointestinal specialist and a few months full of lots of testing, we were still left with no answers. All we knew from the testing and monitors was that Tyler was burping over twelve hundred times a day, with no physiological explanation as to why. His face had become pale, his demeanor was downcast and he struggled to focus in school or enjoy any activities because of the constant burping. I even took him to Dave & Buster's one evening to try to cheer him up, but instead we ended up in the ER because he passed out at the arcade.

By March 2013, Tyler's symptoms had spiraled out of control. His burping had morphed into full-body tics that ripped through him every few seconds. His tics were so extreme that he could not go to sleep because of the constant jerking. That landed us in the hospital, where despite sedatives that could have knocked out a horse, our son's body still could not stop with the tics long enough for him to fall asleep. A week after being admitted to the hospital, he was released with no further answers and enough meds to drop a veil of psychiatric tranquilizers over his mind—but not to stop the tics.

Within the next three weeks, Tyler stopped eating. He became deathly afraid that food was what was causing his illness, so he refused to eat anything. We were able to convince him that he at least needed to drink Ensure and water to stay alive, but he would not even try any of Ensure's different flavors for fear that they would harm him.

He also lost his ability to speak. We noticed that it was getting harder and harder for him to make words out, but at first, we just attributed that to his constant tics and accompanying frustration. On Mother's Day, Tyler came up to Jeanine, and through tics he had a very difficult time getting out the words "Happy Mother's Day." Those three words were the last intelligible words we would hear out of Tyler's mouth for over three months.

I was so frustrated by what Tyler was experiencing, plus I was sick myself, and my mom was dying. I would go to work and be in pain all day long, and then I would come home to a child who was so ill he could not talk or eat or sleep. Tyler used to love to go out on the streets with me to pray for people, but now he could not even leave home. It was in this incredibly low place that I heard the Lord say something surprising: *I want you to pray for the sick as you have never prayed for the sick before. Don't be caught up in the chaos, but be empowered in My commissioning.*

Despite what I was seeing in my own life, Jesus was inviting me to press into more of the Kingdom in healing for others. I determined to pray for the sick at every opportunity. If the enemy was going to hold my family hostage in illness, I was going to make him regret it by ministering Jesus' healing everywhere I could. My friend Robby Dawkins calls this "taking a toll." If the enemy is going to hit my family, I am going to make him pay for it by seeing others be healed and come into the Kingdom.

On several occasions while Tyler was hospitalized, Jeanine and I would see other sick kids in the hospital and take time to pray for them. We left one time to go pick up some fast food, and the woman in the drive-thru was healed of terrible pain in her feet, while our son was across the street at the hospital. Every chance I got, I prayed for people. I continued doing a weekly outreach at a local bingo hall, where we would hand out water and snacks and pray for anyone who would let us. Throughout this time, I saw the most amazing testimonies of God healing other people. Yet nothing was changing with Tyler. In fact, he was getting worse.

Tyler's tics had grown to the point of being dangerous. He was covered in scrapes and bruises because he could not control the way his body would jerk and flail. One terribly timed tic sent him falling down the stairs. He started wearing a helmet to protect his head from unexpected falls. He also yelled constantly and uncontrollably. The yelling tic made it impossible to have quiet for more than just a couple of seconds at a time, and with five other children in the home, that posed quite a challenge.

Most disturbing for me was the change we saw in Tyler's behavior. He became defiant, violent and abusive. Most of his aggression was targeted at me, thankfully, not at his mom or siblings. This sweet boy, who only months before had loved to cuddle up next to me while we played Transformers or watched superhero movies, now attacked me every time I entered the room. This tormented boy whom I loved deeply assaulted me daily with hits, kicks and bites, and I did not know how to help him.

Doctors recommended we institutionalize him, both for his safety and mine. They offered no hope of curing him; we were just advised to institutionalize him, which to me sounded like giving up on him. We refused. Instead, we came up with a plan to keep him at home. My father-in-law began building a padded safe room in our garage for Tyler, where he could go when he was particularly upset. That way, he would not hurt himself or others. We set out to make our home as safe as possible for him, but it would take a while.

Tornado Inside, Tornado Outside

About a year before Tyler became sick, a close friend had given me a prophetic word that did not sound encouraging at all when he gave it, but became a lifeline for me later on. He said, "There are two storms coming, and they are both aiming for your heart. One is from the enemy, and one is from God. It's going to hit your children to get to your heart."

I began to realize that the enemy was using this situation with Tyler to target my heart. The situation was hitting me in all my weak places, and my heart was absolutely broken for him and the destruction our family was experiencing. But at the same time, God was also coming after my heart with His love and comfort.

May in Oklahoma often means tornadoes, and 2013 was no exception. We saw on the news that a tornado was coming in our direction, and thankfully, our other kids were with Jeanine's parents. We knew we could not take Tyler anywhere. He would be too disruptive, and it was nearly impossible to get him to go out. Jeanine and I just looked at each other and shrugged in the silent knowing you gain from fifteen years of marriage. We were both thinking, *How much worse could it be if we got hit by a tornado? The worst tornado ever has already hit. Our life is already in pieces.*

So we had no other choice but to ride out the storm at home. A storm was raging on the inside and a storm was raging on the outside. Sirens were blaring outside, and Tyler was shouting and jerking inside.

God, where are You? my heart cried out in anguish.

Then I had this out-of-place impression from Him: *I want you to go online and watch something.*

Really? I'm in the middle of a tornado! Then I remembered that this same evening, a friend of mine who pastored on the East Coast was going to live stream a guest speaker in his service. When I logged on, the service was nearing the end, and I wondered why I was even watching it.

Suddenly, I felt a deluge of words of knowledge for healing for the people in that service. I thought, *Here I am, in a tornado warning in Oklahoma. My son is in his own tornado, trapped in his brain. And I'm getting words of knowledge for people in another state, where there's peace and calm?* I was perplexed. Was this really the Lord?

I knew the only way I would know for sure was to write down the plethora of words for healing that were coming, and then text them to my pastor friend. At the same time I was sending words of knowledge to my friend, the guest speaker looked perplexed and said, "I'm not sure really how to end the service, because I don't have any leading on how the Lord wants to do ministry. I guess we'll just close the service." This was unusual, because it was not something this man would typically say.

Just then, I saw my pastor friend jump up and grab the mic. "I have a friend in Oklahoma watching this live stream," he said. "The Holy Spirit began to drop words of knowledge for healing to him for people here in this service."

My friend began to read the detailed words of knowledge I had sent, and as each word was read, I saw people standing in response. The live stream ended at that moment, so I was not sure what happened next. About an hour later, I got a call from my friend.

"Man, that was the craziest thing!" he told me. "Every word that you gave, people responded all over the service. Fifty or more people were healed from those words of knowledge."

This doesn't make sense, I thought. *God, You are good! You're at work even in the midst of this storm raging inside and outside. I don't understand what You're doing with Tyler, but I know You're still good and You still heal. Just as You're touching those people on the East Coast, I know You'll touch my son.*

Suddenly, I could feel the comfort of God. Reassurance and faith hit my heart, and I knew that if God would give me words of healing for others, He would also heal my son somehow. In the midst of the two tornadoes, God was going straight after my heart.

Pressing into Hope

Though the outward storm had passed safely, the inward storm within my son, my family and myself raged on. I often struggled with the tormenting emotions of despair, shame and my own pain. I could hear the seducing entrapment of emotional pain trying its best to slither its way back into my thinking. But I just kept submitting to the whisper of hope. Hope started to be easier to hear and pay attention to, even when the winds and waves of doubt were blowing through my emotions. One day in the midst of this struggle I heard the Holy Spirit whisper, *Go downtown.*

Faith hit my heart. I did not know what was downtown, but I knew the Holy Spirit was up to something for my good and His glory. I called my friend Scott, and we both felt as though we should go to the hospital emergency room downtown to love on people. This is something we had often done before.

We went and prayed, loved on and listened to people in the ER as they shared their lives. We saw several people touched power-fully as the Lord gave us prophetic words of encouragement. We saw gripping pain from sickness leave. As we were praying for one guy, a pregnant lady came in screaming, "Help me! Help me! I don't want to lose my baby! I've been in a horrible accident!"

Scott and I ran to her and helped her find her way through the ER to check in. I kept praying for her as she waited for help. I kept speaking peace and letting her know Jesus was right with her. She kept crying out and thanking me for helping. All the nurses were busy elsewhere, and the young lady collapsed in my arms. She had cut marks all over her arms and was in so much pain. She rested her head on my arm and repeated, "I can't lose my baby. It's the only thing I have to live for." Finally, I was able to get her calmed down and checked in.

Walking back through the ER, I passed a lady whom the Lord gave me a word about. It involved a condition in her back, and I shared it with her. She said, "That's why I'm in the ER!"

Scott and I prayed for her. She had one leg shorter than the other from an accident, and she and her friend watched as it grew out right before their eyes. She was so shocked that all her pain was gone! We shared the Gospel with her and found out she was in a mission home and was trying to turn her life around. We prayed over her as the presence of the Lord came upon her. It was so sweet. She could not believe what had happened.

As we left her, we saw another woman in severe pain. We asked if we could pray for her. She nodded. Clenching her teeth, she whispered, "I'm having back spasms." Tears of pain and fear rolled down her cheeks. Scott and I spoke to the pain, and we watched as it began to leave. She kept saying, "Thank You, Jesus. Thank You." The pain receded enough for her to sit down. We prayed more and loved on her. The spasm pain left. Then we prayed for the sharp pain in her kidneys and watched it leave. A deep peace came over her—so much so that she started to fall asleep. She just kept thanking Jesus. It was amazing.

As we walked out, Scott and I found a few more people to pray for. We watched the Lord come and touch people and take away their pain. As we left the building, I saw two women standing out front, in an area where patients who were able could come outside to get some fresh air. I asked if I could pray for them. One of the ladies said, "Please pray for me. I have terminal cancer and two other really painful conditions. My pain is off the charts!"

I began to pray, and the presence of the Lord came upon her. I had to hold her up several times so she would not fall. She kept feeling surges of power and heat go through her body as the pain left her. She told me she could feel the warmth and tingling, and she was so amazed. I told her this was the love of Jesus, and I asked where her faith was. She said, "Oh, I love Him!" I asked her if I could give her a hug. She leaned into me and said yes. Then she walked back to her room with no pain.

Afterward, Scott and I decided to hang out at a local pub for a bit. While we were there, the Holy Spirit spoke to me about a condition in one guy's back. I approached him, and he was so taken aback that I knew what was going on with him. I prayed, "Thank You, Jesus, for healing his back."

The presence of God came all over this guy so tangibly that he fell onto our table, shaking under the power of God. "The pain is all gone!" he exclaimed. "I just had a God encounter!"

"Yes, you're right!" I said. "You just had a God encounter."

I had started my day in a battle, with the enemy pulling me toward despair. When you find yourself in this kind of war, be careful not to put your focus on him. He loves the attention. You might feel strong at first focusing on the enemy, as if you are really kicking it to him, but it is a trap. You need to put your focus on God, not on him. The best way to fight is to submit to God and resist the enemy, and then he will flee. You war by submitting, resisting, worshiping God and remembering who He is and who you are. The best way to submit and resist is to go be what God has called you to be—hope for the hopeless.

We all struggle through things, and we have the choice to stay paralyzed and defeated in that struggle, or to become hope for those around us who are as desperate for hope and healing as we are. We are all wounded healers, but we don't have to be hopeless victims. Stepping out of our hopelessness may be the key that opens the door for someone else to experience a God encounter. As you choose to be a voice of hope to the hopeless, you will find yourself strengthened in His hope flowing through you.

Kingdom Justice

During this time, plans were underway at our house to build that safe room for Tyler where he could have his toys and even a new television and game console. The padded walls and floor would keep him from injuring himself, and it would be a safe place to put him when he was raging, so he could not hurt himself or me. My father-in-law drew up the plans to build the room into our garage and accommodate it with heat and air conditioning. A few friends came into town for the weekend to help on the construction.

The afternoon when the work began was one of my lowest moments. Tyler flew into another rage and started attacking me again. He was pounding his fists into the top of my head, and I was doing my best to protect myself. This was not Tyler. He was sick.

I broke down that day. My father-in-law pulled Tyler off me and took him to another room, and afterward I sat at my dining room table, placed my head into my hands and just began to weep. I was devastated. *God, where are You?*

Through my sobs, I could pick up on pieces of the conversation happening around the table between Jeanine, my in-laws and my friends. They were brainstorming ideas for how to keep both Tyler and me safe until we could get the safe room built. They were having trouble coming up with ideas about how to restrain him in a dignifying way.

"What if we had some sort of soft wrist restraint that could be connected to a belt around his waist when he's in these fits of rage? That way he doesn't hurt himself or his dad," someone suggested.

"Where would you find soft hand restraints?"

"I know this sounds odd, but what about the soft kind of restraints you can get at a sex shop?" someone asked.

"That just might work!" another said.

A sex shop? I thought. I could not believe my son's health had deteriorated to the point where I was even listening to such a conversation in my home.

In the middle of my despair, with tears rolling down my face as I heard them talking about a sex shop—at that very moment, I saw an open vision come into my mind. I saw a woman standing in a particular sex shop in our city. She was in terrible pain because of an accident. *Am I going out of my mind*, I wondered, *or is this Jesus?* I had a choice to make. *Am I going to respond to what I sense Jesus showing me, or am I going to stay bound in my despair?*

I heard someone volunteer to visit the shop to see about finding something that would work for Tyler. I did not tell anyone about the vision, but I spoke up for the first time through my tears. "No, Jeanine and I can go get what we need for Tyler."

Some friends offered to come with us. When the four of us arrived at the store, a woman greeted us as we walked in. "Well hello, Superman. What can I help you with?" she said to me.

I looked down to see that I was wearing a Superman T-shirt. I also noticed that my friend was wearing another superhero shirt. Apparently, the Justice League had just walked into the sex shop. I started to try to explain why we were there. "This is going to sound extremely strange. . . ." Not wanting her to misunderstand my motives for being at the store, I quickly described Tyler's situation.

"Oh, how sad!" she said. "I can't imagine what you're going through. But I think I can find something that will work." She started showing us different options and giving us ideas.

Again, I could not help but think to myself how insane this entire situation was. After we found something for Tyler, we went to check out. One of my friends said to the woman, "I bet this is one of the oddest things you've dealt with in this store."

"Yeah, this is unusual, but I've seen a lot of strange things," she said.

At that moment, I recognized that this was the woman I had seen in my vision. From the beginning, I had been pretty sure she was the person, but honestly, we were focused at first on getting what we needed for Tyler. Once that was taken care of, I could shift my attention to her.

"I think it's about to get a lot stranger," I said. She looked at me, puzzled, as I went on. "You were in an accident, and you've suffered a major injury that causes you tremendous pain. Would you like me to take care of that pain?"

She looked at me in shock. "How did you know? And how can you take care of it?"

"I sometimes get pictures and impressions for people. How much pain are you in right now?"

"I'm in horrible pain, even after taking two pain pills an hour ago. Normally, my pain is off the charts."

"Let me see your hand," I said as I extended mine to her. She took my hand as I prayed, "Holy Spirit, let Your healing come upon this woman's body. I break the power of this pain now."

Then I watched as her whole body trembled. The tangible presence of the Holy Spirit began to heal her.

"What's going on?" she asked as she felt His waves of love and power coursing through her.

"Move your body around and look for the pain."

As she did, she could not find any more pain. Her face and tears said it all. She looked at me and said, "Who are you?"

I smiled and said, "I'm Superman. Don't you remember?" We both laughed. I added, "What you just experienced was Jesus healing your body. He loves you so much that He showed me a picture of you while I was at home, sitting at my dining room table, crying and wondering what to do for my son. Jesus led me to your store to find you."

"You're a Christian?!" she said in bewilderment. I could immediately tell from her tone that she had had some unpleasant interactions with Christians.

"Yes, I am. But I'm not the kind of Christian you're thinking about. I'm not going to beat you over the head with a Bible. If Jesus were here today walking around, guess where He would be? He would be right here with you. He would walk right into your shop to find you and set you free. That's the Jesus I know."

Let me back up to something that had happened a few days earlier. Part of Tyler's illness involved obsessive-compulsive thoughts. He had woken up one morning particularly agitated, flinging himself all over the room, pounding his hands onto the floor and yelling more than usual. Jeanine tried calming him and asked, "Are you having bad thoughts you can't control?" He frantically nodded yes. "Can you try to tell me what it's about?" she asked. He used his finger to spell out on the ground s-e-x.

The enemy had been using my nine-year-old son's ill brain to torment him with intrusive sexual thoughts and images. Yet here we were in a sex shop, bringing healing and the Gospel to a woman who was also tormented in her own kind of bondage. That day we became God's Justice League, bringing justice to the same area in which the enemy was trying to torment my son. We did it by setting a woman free. Kingdom justice was being served. God was taking what the enemy meant for evil and my son's destruction and turning it right around as Jesus sent His Kingdom Justice League to set a woman free and plunder the enemy's kingdom.

The Kingdom of God is at hand at the craziest and most difficult times, but I have found it does not always look the way we want it to look. And that brings up in us the *why* question. We are all going to go through times that are tough and that challenge our faith. How are we going to respond? We can let the hook of the *why* question come so deep into our souls that it drives us down, bound by the circumstances. Or we can be like the psalmist, who cried out, "Why, my soul, are you downcast? Why so disturbed within me? Put your hope in God" (Psalm 42:5, 11). That is a great question to ask. Rather than asking God why, turn that question toward your downcast soul. God is still good. God is still in control. God still has a plan. Put your hope in God!

God is so good that He can reveal His goodness even in the darkest and most evil of times. There are things we can only learn and experience about the nature of God during the valley of the shadow of death. It is one thing to know God is the Comforter; it is another thing to be comforted by God. Rather than asking why, we can instead ask, *What is this for? What are You wanting to show me and be for me now that You couldn't be for me before?* Jesus wants to show Himself faithful to you in every situation. He is Immanuel, the God who is with you, especially in your darkest and weakest hour.

The Mission Never Stops

Jesus did not call us to partner with Him on mission only when life is good. His mission never stops. Yes, there are times when what that looks like must change, but as long as we are on this earth, we are in partnership with Christ to accomplish His purposes. At the children's hospital, I was able to pray with people whom I never would have met if my son had not been a patient. There are those whom we can comfort only because we have walked the same desperate journey they are on. The way we engage in His mission may be altered, but the commission is still the same. Proclaim the Good News, heal the sick, cast out demons, cleanse the lepers and raise the dead (see Matthew 10:7–8 once more).

After months of misdiagnosis and incorrect medical treatment that was actually making things worse, we finally met Dr. Stanbro, who said the best two sentences of my life: "I know what this is. And I know how to fix it."

Tyler was diagnosed with PANDAS, which stands for Pediatric Autoimmune Neuropsychiatric Disorder Associated with Streptococcus. That really long phrase means Tyler had a strep infection that his immune system responded to incorrectly, causing an autoimmune encephalitis. Rather than his immune system fighting off the strep bacteria, it instead created proteins that damaged his brain. The results were extreme tics, obsessive-compulsive disorder, anxiety and behavioral changes.

The doctor wanted to place Tyler on high-dose antibiotics to fight the bacteria and heal the inflammation wreaking havoc in his brain. This was wonderful news, but it was not going to be an overnight turnaround. We still had months of struggle—maybe longer—before we would see Tyler slowly come out from underneath the haze of illness. In the meantime, all we could do was pray and hope the doctor was right.

During the height of Tyler's illness, some friends from church paid for us to have a night away, with dinner and a hotel, so we could rest and recoup a little while Jeanine's parents stayed with Tyler and our other kids. Jeanine and I went to one of our favorite restaurants to spend most of the evening in quiet, simply enjoying being away from the chaos and noisy shouts that had filled our last several months at home. The quiet also gave me an opportunity to listen to what the Father was doing in and around me.

As the waitress was serving our dessert, I said, "Do you mind if I share something with you?"

"Sure," she said.

"Sometimes I get pictures and impressions for people's lives," I told her. "Do you mind if I share with you what I see?" I could sense her intrigue. I began to tell her what I saw, and I continued for several minutes as the Lord gave me more prophetic encouragement for her.

She began to weep openly, saying, "You have such a gift. Everything you said was correct."

I told her, "I'm not sure what your experience has been with churches or with Jesus. I'm His follower, and sometimes the Church has done a poor job of expressing His heart and ways. But this is Jesus' heart for you. He knows you and has destiny over your life."

"I don't know what to say. All you're saying is true," she said. She was so undone. "I haven't been in a church or prayed for years. Just a few days ago, I prayed for the first time in ages. Then you share all this with me."

I then went on to encourage her, "In these last few years, Jesus hasn't been bothered by your questions and wrestling, nor has He turned His heart from you. Rather, He has fixed His gaze intensely toward you. This is a message of His love and destiny over your life."

She thanked us profusely, and she turned and walked away with tears running down her cheeks and hope beaming from her countenance. The justice of God was breaking in for this beautiful lady, even while we were still struggling under our own pain and conflict.

Several months later, Jeanine and I visited the same restaurant again to celebrate our sixteenth anniversary. Tyler was still very sick, but we were beginning to see small but significant signs of improvement. A few weeks before our anniversary, he had started talking again. I can't tell you how sweet the first words of a healing child are! His tics were still constant, but they were less extreme. His anxiety and OCD were still out of control. He had even tried running away from home a few times. He had constant bouts of defiance and rage, but he was not attacking me as often as he had earlier. He had not eaten any food yet, either, and he also still refused to touch anyone or be touched by anyone. We had no idea when or if he would be able to start going back to school. We were still so far away from any kind of normal life with him. The day-after-day, nonstop struggle was a burden to us, so we appreciated any chance we had to get away, even if only for a few hours.

While we were at the restaurant, we saw the same waitress who had served us before. She came up to our table and immediately said, "Can I give you a hug?" She began to tell us how the night we prayed and shared destiny words over her had changed her life, and her cousin's life, forever. Now they are both living for Jesus. They go to church, pray and read their Bibles every night, and God has radically changed them. "I feel goose bumps all over just talking about it!" she said. I could tell she was on the verge of tears.

A little while later our waitress this time, a different one, said, "That's really cool! My friend told me back in the kitchen that you were the couple from a few months ago. She had told me back then how you had done this amazing reading on her. Is that what you call it? A reading?"

Jeanine and I looked at each other and smiled. Then I said, "You could call it that. We just think of it as how Jesus knows your heart and has really great things to say, and He really loves people."

"Are you ministers or something?" she asked.

"No, we're just followers of Jesus."

Before this conversation even happened, she had mentioned her boyfriend, and at that time I had gotten an impression that he had a sports injury in his shoulder and back, but I had not shared it yet. So the next time she came over, I asked, "Does your boyfriend have pain in his shoulder and back?"

"I don't know, but he's really athletic, so he has lots of sports injuries."

"When you see him next, put your hand on his shoulder and say, 'Jesus heals you. Pain, leave,' and Jesus will heal him."

"That's awesome. I will!" When she brought us our check, she said, "I couldn't wait till I got home. I texted him to see if his shoulder and back are hurting. He hasn't texted me back, but I hope he does. I'm really curious!" We were excited to see her anticipation about what God would do.

I am so thankful now for those simple words I heard from God: *I want you to pray for the sick as you have never prayed for the sick before. Don't be caught up in the chaos, but be empowered in My commissioning.*

Press into the commission, no matter what your circumstances. Stay on mission, even if right now the way you walk in that mission looks different than usual.

The Road to Healing

I would love to say that God miraculously intervened and healed Tyler in a moment, but that is not how it has happened. God is healing Tyler, but it is coming through doctors, medications, lots of hard work and prayer. All healing is from God, and healing through medical professionals is not second-class healing.

It has now been six years since Tyler's symptoms first started. He no longer suffers from tics, and he loves eating at McDonald's a little too much. But life is still a challenge for him. He struggles daily with anxiety and OCD. To help reduce the anxiety, we have moved him out of the traditional schoolroom into a home-based charter school. He also goes to group and individual therapy weekly to help him deal with the stress and anxiety that try to overwhelm him.

The Tyler we see today, however, is a world away from the scared little boy trapped in a body and brain he could not control. He has a hilarious wit, and his creativity and intelligence are astounding. He loves playing chess and video games. And best of all, his compassionate and sensitive personality is back, and all signs of illness-induced anger and rage are gone. Not only that, but because

Tyler's case was so extreme and so many medical professionals were involved in his care, his recovery shed new light on PANDAS. Since Tyler's experience, dozens of other kids in our area have now been correctly diagnosed and treated, and they are recovering. God uses all things for good!

And that boy loves to pray for people. Everywhere we go, he asks if he can tell people about Jesus or pray for healing. He loves to research different faiths so he can explain the Gospel better to people from various religious backgrounds. And the level of the prophetic and words of knowledge he operates in is astoundingly specific and accurate. Last summer, I took him with me on a ministry trip and was looking forward to spending an evening doing nothing after driving all day. Tyler, however, wanted to go pray for people. When I protested that I just wanted to relax in the hotel room, Tyler said, "I don't know about you, Daddy, but I take praying for people very seriously!" I couldn't help but laugh. *I've created a monster*, I thought to myself.

Also, since 2013 other things have changed. My esophageal illness continued to escalate, and God healed me through surgery in 2014. My mom had surgery for her cancer, and it went into remission. She had a new lease on life, but the time the surgery bought her eventually came to an end and she started deteriorating as the cancer found its way back. She lived in constant, tremendous pain, and she began losing weight. Her cancer treatments were taking a toll on her body, with no sign of improvement. By the summer of 2017, she had dwindled down to a meager 97 pounds.

I began to realize that my remaining time with my mom on earth was probably very limited. She had never been to an ocean, so Jeanine and I decided to invite her on a road trip with the family. It would be one last opportunity for her to walk along a beach and spend a few days watching her grandkids play in the ocean. She gladly accepted. While the trip was difficult for her, it was also fun to see her smile and feel the ocean across her toes for the first time in her life.

On our drive home, we made an unexpected stop at a hotel because the long car ride was taking a toll on my mom. That night, I asked my three boys to circle around her and pray. To my surprise, a boldness came over Tyler as the boys prayed. "I speak to that cancer and I command it to go!" he said. Then he proclaimed with authority and conviction, "Nana, I believe when you go back to the doctor, you'll have no more cancer, and you won't have to do any more treatments."

I was shocked. And I must admit, I was not nearly as full of faith as Tyler was. A couple of weeks later, I was at a conference when I got a text from my sister. She had taken my mom to the oncologist to hear the results of her latest PET scan. There was no more sign of cancer, and the doctor had told her she could stop all the treatments. The doctor had even used the word *miracle* to describe her recovery. Tyler's prayer had been answered. God had healed my mom through this boy who had experienced so much pain and healing of his own.

Finding Identity in Christ

Rather than being defined by our circumstances, weaknesses and deficits, our identity lies only in Jesus, who bought us for a price. Don't forget who you are, and you won't act like who you are not. Breathe in a fresh revelation of the nature and mercy of an amazing God who made and transformed you into His likeness. Live from the vine of life, Jesus, who is the way, the truth and the life. He chose you. He redeemed you. He created you, so don't be who you are not, but be who He says you are. Then you will live like He is and do what He does. You are a reflection of His radiant beauty, a messenger of hope and reconciliation.

May heaven invade our earthly minds so that we might live out the gospel of God's goodness and bring hope and resurrection to those in the shadows of death. You are the righteousness of God in Christ Jesus, not by your good works, but because of His glorious work and grace. So go and enjoy the Good News, and share it by drinking from it first. Then let it flow out of you, causing others to taste and see that He is good. His goodness leads transgressors into sonship. God is not mad at you, so stop being mad at yourself, the world and others. Instead, be who He has called you to be—a reformer full of hope and joy in chaos. His life is living bread. Take a bite and see. And share the Bread of Life you are feasting on. Though you have feet of clay, there is a treasure of hope and life in you. It is Jesus, and He is the Good News the world is searching for.

A HEALING AND POWER EVANGELISM MODEL

When we look at how Jesus did ministry, we see that He used a huge variety of methods. He did everything from commanding the sickness to leave, to casting out demons, to releasing forgiveness that causes healing, to spitting in a man's eyes. Clearly, there was no single method He used to make healing happen. The only common thread is that under the empowerment of the Holy Spirit, Jesus did what He saw the Father doing. There is no such thing as a magic formula that makes healing, deliverance or salvation happen, or that brings forth a prophetic word for someone. Rather, the common thread is dependence on the Holy Spirit rather than on ourselves, on various models or on any other human construct.

Alexander Venter says in his book *Doing Healing: How to Minister God's Kingdom in the Power of the Spirit*,

> Conference after conference repeatedly taught the "how to", but I slowly realised that *it was not about methods and technique, but about means and purpose.* Healing and miracles do not happen because we do one, two, and three. If it genuinely happens, it is

because of the gracious presence and mysterious power *of God*—not because of the man/woman of God, or the right way of doing it.

. . . Jesus did not model a method or technique; he modelled kingdom ministry. . . . Learning to heal the sick and minister the kingdom is not about "how to's"—it is about learning to walk on water—all the best methods will not keep you afloat! The ability to transcend the laws of nature is not discovered by mastering spiritual laws, principles and techniques. It is about raw faith in God.[1]

The model I explain in this chapter is not meant to be a formula. It is meant to be a starting point that gives you handholds to hang on to in following the Holy Spirit's leading. The goal is to respond to the Spirit, not to stick to this model. The model simply gives you steps to take to help you hear and respond to the Spirit.

Furthermore, it is important to note that every follower of Jesus is unique. We all have our unique blend of spiritual gifting, calling, personality and history with God. As you try this model, there will be parts of it that really resonate with you and other parts that don't fit you. This model is meant to be a starting point for you to experiment with and then make your own. In fact, much of what I have included here is my own variation of John Wimber's 5-step healing model, which I have modified for on-the-streets power evangelism that works for me. Feel free to use what works for you and adapt what does not.

The five steps I use for this healing and power evangelism model are to *approach*, *ask*, *pray*, *assess* and *explain*. Let's look at each of these a little more closely.

Step 1: Approach

The approach is usually the hardest step. When approaching someone, always follow the way of love. Cultivate values that set people

---

1. Alexander Venter, *Doing Healing: How to Minister God's Kingdom in the Power of the Spirit* (South Africa: Kingdom Treasures, 2017), 100.

at ease and demonstrate the love and power of our good God. Remember that you are serving the one you are ministering to. Treat the person with respect and honor.

When you approach someone, have faith in Jesus' commission to heal the sick and have confidence in His present activity in that person's life. Be friendly, and smile! Introduce yourself and ask the person's name, just as you would any other time. All approaches involve risk, so nothing will stop the butterflies in your stomach. But risk opens the door to the impossible.

You can approach someone in a number of ways. I call this first way the "Can I pray for you?" approach. You can use this approach anytime, anywhere. You simply ask people if you can pray for them for any physical or spiritual needs they have. This does not require you to observe a need or receive a word of knowledge beforehand. The only requirement is having a heart of love and taking a risk.

The second way is the "visible need" approach. This is when you see or hear of a need that you can offer to pray for. If you see someone walking with a crutch, you could say, "I noticed that you have a crutch. You look as if you're in pain. What happened?" I have found that people often love to share about their lives, and they enjoy a listening ear.

The third type of approach is with a word of knowledge. This is when you feel you have received information from God that you could not have known outside His revelation. This could be a word of knowledge for physical healing or a prophetic word of destiny for someone's life. It could involve knowing things such as someone's dreams, talents, challenges or needs. Sharing a word of knowledge can stir faith for the person to receive healing and the love of God. For example, you could say, "Sometimes I get pictures and impressions for people about physical needs or things going on in their lives. Would you like me to share what I sensed for you?"

This approach often evokes curiosity and invites conversation. If the person is interested, then you can share the impression you had. Don't give up if you get the word of knowledge or an impression wrong. It is okay to miss it. Missing it can be the icebreaker that leads to a spiritual conversation. You can then ask if the person has any needs you can pray for.

A word of knowledge can come in several ways. You can *see it* as a picture in your mind or an open-eyed vision. You can *feel it*, such as feeling a sympathy pain in your body that is not your own pain. Likewise, you can feel an emotion that is not your own emotion. You can also *think it*, such as hearing a word or phrase internally, or having a subtle thought or an inner knowing that something is true. Most words of knowledge are quick, fleeting impressions rather than something that feels overwhelming or certain.

You can approach people in an infinite number of ways. Your approach will vary, depending on the setting and the person you are approaching. Be creative and customize an approach that is uniquely yours. Develop your own style that flows from your personality.

Step 2: Ask

After you have approached a person and introduced yourself, the next step is to ask. Ask him or her questions to find out some basic information about the condition or situation you will be praying for. Listen for responses on two planes: Listen to the person, and listen to the Holy Spirit for revelatory insight.

When talking about a physical pain or ailment, ask people how long they have had it and if they know what caused it. If they are in pain, I like to have them rate the pain on a scale from zero to ten, with ten being the worst. This indicator can help us know how much pain a person is in, and it gives us an indicator of how well our prayers are working as we find out if the pain is decreasing.

Ask if you can pray for someone's condition or situation right away. When praying for healing, it is often helpful to lay hands on the afflicted area, if that is appropriate and if the situation is conducive to doing so. But always ask permission before you touch a person. If people seem uneasy about you touching or praying for them, you could say, "No one has to know we are praying. I'll simply keep my eyes open and pray, just as if we are having a conversation."

If people refuse prayer, honor their wishes and pray on your own later. Thank them and let them know Jesus loves them. But unless you strongly feel the Lord telling you otherwise, don't push a conversation or prayer on someone who does not want it.

Step 3: Pray

Prayer is often actually the shortest part of the 5-step model. Remember that in public settings, you usually only have fifteen to thirty seconds to pray for someone. It has been my experience that half a minute is all the time you will have, because the people you approach are already busy doing something or going somewhere. If God starts moving, they will often stop what they are doing and a longer conversation between you can develop. Yet if you start with a long, wordy prayer, you often lose the person's interest up front, and you won't get far. If you start by praying quickly, full of faith and in authority, God often moves quickly. So use quick prayers of command to begin with, not long, petitioning prayers. Jesus' prayers were often very short prayers of command such as "rise up and walk" or "be healed." Invite the presence of the Holy Spirit to come. When praying for healing, speak to the pain or condition and tell it to go.

Step 4: Assess

Immediately after you pray, ask people what they are experiencing. When praying for healing, ask them what their pain level is or ask them to move in a way that they could not move before, to test out the effectiveness of the prayer. People may experience relief of their symptoms, warmth, tingling, coolness or a sense of God's presence or peace. They may also experience nothing.

Point out indicators of God's activity, such as signs of healing or of His presence. This keeps people engaged in the prayer process. For example, you could say something like, "You said the pain started at an eight, but now it's a six. That's amazing! If it went down to a six, I believe it can go to a zero. Do you mind if I pray again?"

After assessing the situation, go back to Step 3 and pray again if healing is incomplete—as long as the person agrees to more prayer. You can stop praying when the condition has been fully healed, when a person indicates that he or she is done receiving prayer or when you sense the Holy Spirit telling you the prayer time is over.

Step 5: Explain

Without some explanation, people will not always draw the correct conclusions from the experience they have when you pray for them. Afterward, tell them that what they experienced was Jesus coming near them because He is real and He loves them. If they experienced any measure of healing, tell them, "What God did in your body, He wants to do in your whole life."

Explain the Gospel to people in simple terms, avoiding Christian jargon they would not understand. Invite them to meet with you again, such as for coffee or a meal. Explain how they can connect more with Jesus, such as through reading the Bible or getting involved in a local church.

When sharing the Gospel by demonstration and proclamation, we are only responsible for giving the invitation. We are not responsible for a person's response. James Engel has developed a tool called the Engel Scale to represent the process people go through in response to Christ. Though his full scale includes more steps, basically people go from an ignorance of Christ, to an awareness of Christ, to an understanding of Christ, to a personal involvement with Christ, to an eventual decision for Christ. Some people take this journey very slowly. For other people, a power encounter such as a healing can move them very quickly through the scale. Our job is simply to help them move farther down the scale, and often that involves inviting them into a decision for salvation.

There are a great many models for explaining the Gospel to others in a simple but effective way. Three of the best I have seen used extremely effectively are "Jesus at the Door" by Scott McNamara, "Miracle Question" by Mark Marx and "Three Circles" by Jimmy Scroggins and Steve Wright. You can look up all three online for more information.[2] When we invite someone to open his or her heart to Jesus, we need to remember that there is no magical prayer for that person to pray that seals the deal of eternal destiny. The Bible simply says that if people believe in their hearts that God raised Jesus from the dead and confess with their mouths that Jesus is Lord, they will be saved. It also says that all who call on the name of the Lord will be saved (see Romans 10:9, 13). We simply want to help people confess with their mouths and call on the Lord.

If people are ready to receive Christ, it is helpful to model for them a short prayer for salvation. Using a prayer like this one, you can ask them to pray after you or with you:

Jesus, thank You for revealing Your love and presence to me. If You can heal my broken body, I believe You can heal my broken life. I believe You died on the cross for me, to deliver me from evil and sin. Jesus, I no longer want to live my own

---

2. See more about "Jesus at the Door" by Scott McNamara at www.jesusatthedoor.com. See more about "Miracle Question" by Mark Marx at www.healingonthestreets.com. See more about "Three Circles" by Jimmy Scroggins and Steve Wright in their book *Turning Everyday Conversations into Gospel Conversations* (B&H Books, 2016), and at www.lifeonmissionbook.com.

way. I want to live out Your original design for my life. Would You come fill me with the Holy Spirit and empower me to live for You, so that my life puts You on display?

Workers for the Harvest Field

Once again, the five steps in this healing and power evangelism model are to *approach*, *ask*, *pray*, *assess* and *explain*. Taking these five steps has worked well for me in doing power evangelism on the streets. Give them a try, adapting them to fit your personality and making them your own, so that they work for you.

Jesus told His disciples in Matthew 9:37–38: "The harvest is plentiful but the workers are few. Ask the Lord of the harvest, therefore, to send out workers into his harvest field."

The harvest is waiting out there, and the results will amaze you when you use this 5-step model to approach people and put Jesus on display for them with love and power!

Brian Blount has spent the last twenty years equipping and training individuals, teams and churches in healing and power evangelism. He is a graphic designer and church planter. Brian is passionate about living a lifestyle of putting Jesus on display with love and power, and equipping others to do the same.

Brian has been a part of the Vineyard movement for over twenty years and has ministered extensively in Vineyard churches throughout the United States, Europe and South Africa. He has been a speaker at the Vineyard USA national conference and More Love More Power conferences. Brian has also ministered internationally in Russia, Germany, Switzerland, Romania, the Netherlands, Slovakia, Brazil and South Africa.

Brian and his wife, Jeanine, are currently senior pastors of Crestwood Vineyard Church in Oklahoma City, Oklahoma, where they live with their six children, three of whom are triplets.